CU00764270

NUFFIELD
ECONOMICS
& BUSINESS

Poverty and Wealth

Is inequality inevitable?

HERSCHEL GRAMMAR SCHOOL
NORTHAMPTON AVENUE
SLOUGH SL1 3BW

LONGMAN

Copyright acknowledgements

The Nuffield Economics and Business Project team and the Publishers are grateful to the following for permission to reproduce copyright material:

The Body Shop International plc for extracts from *Trade Not Aid Fact Sheets*; The Economist for extracts from © *The Economist*, 2.10.1993, 18.12.1993, 15.1.1994, 19.2.1994, 26.2.1994, 5.3.1994; The Financial Times for extracts from *The European*, 16.9.1993 and *The Financial Times*, 28.9.1993; Oxfam UK for an extract from *The Trade Trap* by Belinda Coote, published by Oxfam UK and Ireland, Oxford UK, 1992; Newspaper Publishing plc for extracts from *Independent on Sunday*, 13.2.1994 and 26.9.1993; Newsweek International for an extract from *Newsweek Program* © 1991 by Jonathan Kozol; Times Newspapers Ltd for extracts from *The Times*, 31.10.1993, 21.11.1993, 6.1.1994; United Nations Information Centre for extracts from *Human Development Report*, 1992 and 1993.

Thanks are also due to the following for permission to reproduce figures:

Central Statistical Office for Figures 1.9, 1.18, 4.2, 5.6, 5.7, 5.8, 5.9; *The Economist* for Figure 5.12; European Parliament for Figures 5.16 and 5.17; Harrington Kilbride, Employmant Gazette and Department of Employment for Figures 1.19, 1.20, 1.21, 1.22, 1.23; HMSO for Figure 1.24 which is used by permission of the Controller of Her Majesty's Stationery Office; International Monetary Fund for Figure 3.8; London School of Economics for Figures 5.10, 5.11; OECD for Figures 3.7, 3.8; ODA for Enquiry 2 opening evidence; Oxfam and Oxford Cartographers for Figure 1.6; Oxford University Press for Figures 1.15, 2.3; Oxford University Press, New York for Figures 1.2, 1.3, 1.4, 1.5, 1.7, 1.8, 1.13, 1.14, 1.16, 1.17, 2.1, 2.7, 2.8, 3.10, 3.12, 4.6; Joseph Rowntree Foundation and London School of Economics for Figure 5.13; US Department of Labor for Figure 3.9; World Bank for Figures 1.1, 1.14, 2.2, 2.3, 2.4, 2.5, 3.1, 3.2, 3.4, 3.7, 3.11, 4.1, 4.3, 4.4, 4.5, 4.8, 4.9, 4.10, 5.2, 5.3, 5.4, 5.5, Enquiry 1 opening evidence, Enquiry 4 opening evidence.

Acknowledgement is also due to the following for permission to reproduce illustrations on the pages indicated:

Earthscan for pp. 9 and 51; Ron Giling and Panos Pictures for p. 49; Paul Harrison and Panos Pictures for p. 62; H. Kanus and Barnabys Picture Library for p. 75; Oxfam for p. 37; Alan Reininger and The Telegraph Colour Library for p. 34; Sean Sprague and Panos Pictures for pp. 66 and 78; The Telegraph Colour Library for p. 27.

The Publishers have been unable to trace the copyright holders of the cartoons on pp. 25 and 36 and would welcome any additional information.

Longman Group Limited
Longman House, Burnt Mill,
Harlow, Essex, CM20 2JE, England
and Associated Companies throughout the world.

© The Nuffield Foundation 1995

All rights reserved. No part of this publication may be reproduced, stored in a retrieval system, or transmitted in any form or by any means, electronic, mechanical, photocopying, recording, or otherwise without the prior written permission of the Publishers or a licence permitting restricted copying issued by the Copyright Licensing Agency Ltd, 90 Tottenham Court Road, London, W1P 9HE.

ISBN 0 582 24579 6

First published 1995

Designed and typeset by
Ken Vail Graphic Design, Cambridge

Printed in Singapore by Longman
Singapore Publishers Pte Ltd

The Publisher's policy is to use paper manufactured from sustainable forests.

Contents

About this book

Introduction

Poverty and Wealth: Is inequality inevitable? is composed of five Enquiries, which investigate the subject in an integrated manner. As inequality is present in all parts of the world, each Enquiry takes a global perspective and incorporates material from both the developed and developing world to provide a backdrop for the application of economic principles. To assist in the process of enquiry, relevant concepts and ideas are highlighted by notes in the margin of the book.

Economic concepts are put to work in these Enquiries. Ideas of opportunity cost, supply and demand and elasticity are the starting points. From here you will be expected to use aggregate demand and supply, production possibility frontiers and comparative advantage combined with the idea of trade-offs.

Enquiry guide

The questions

Each Enquiry is intended to take about two weeks of the course and will be guided by the questions that introduce each section. The diagrammatic form of these questions shows how they relate to each other and therefore gives structure to the Enquiry. They are not, however, exhaustive and there will be further questions to ask, depending on how your enquiry develops. One strategy is to look at each question in turn and ask whether there are any subsidiary ones that relate to it. Having done this, you will need to put them into a coherent form and the following guidelines should assist you:

- How are these questions related to each other?
- Which questions are most important?
- Can the questions be answered with the information available?
- What other information will be needed to draw conclusions?

The opening evidence

The opening evidence should be used, together with the questions, to set your agenda. It presents points of view that demonstrate a range of perspectives on the problem in hand and provides a starting point for investigation. You may agree with some of it, or you may disagree, but to come to a reasoned conclusion, the different angles should be explored.

The evidence is not exhaustive and will be followed up in the text. There will also be other sources which you may wish to use as reference.

The text

The text forms the main body of the book and underpins the Enquiry. In general, it does not answer all the questions, but it provides a good deal of information that can be used to come to conclusions. By applying your knowledge of economics to the evidence, you will be using the techniques of the economist.

You will find 'Open Questions' in the margin. These are questions that do not have a simple answer but which should be considered carefully. They relate to issues on which no real agreement can be expected because an individual's views will depend upon personal values. By discussing the questions you will be able to identify the breadth of the argument.

It is important to remember that you are being given a source of information rather than an analysis of the problems and solutions of inequality. Your enquiry will enable you to explore and develop your understanding and form your own ideas.

Other sources

You will need to consult a range of other sources in order to carry out your investigation. Books, periodicals, newspapers and databases will all prove useful. If you have access to IT databases and CD-ROM you will find these helpful. Updating information will be an essential part of your enquiry as economics never stands still.

The outcome

The outcome of an Enquiry will be an analysis of the issues you have explored and an evaluation of the problems of inequality that face countries and the world as a whole. You will be able to look at existing strategies for dealing with the problems and evaluate their outcomes. Perhaps you will even be able to make some suggestions about improving things in future. Ideally you should find that these Enquiries have laid the foundations for evaluating future trends as they hit the headlines.

The options and the course

This book is one of a series which has been developed by the Nuffield Economics and Business Project to support Nuffield A levels in Economics and Business. These courses are examined by London Examinations. Although written for a particular course, the book may be useful to anyone studying A level Economics or who is interested in the subject.

The Nuffield courses in Economics and Business have six options, which follow that part of the course common to all. This book covers Option 1. If it is studied with Option 2 *Government Objectives: Can we control the economy?* it leads to an A level in Economics. It can also be combined with any of the other four options, so leading to a joint A level in Economics and Business.

Acknowledgements

This book was written by Jenny Wales.

We are grateful to Nicholas O'Flynn, Alan Hamlin, Julian LeGrande and Marisol Smith for their very considerable help in reading and commenting on early versions of the book.

NANCY WALL
Editor

Enquiry 1: How unequal is the world?

Scope

The world is a very unequal place. This enquiry aims to identify the varying degrees of inequality, both between and within countries. To achieve a broader understanding of the issue, various facets are explored, including the meaning of the term inequality and the interpretation of relevant data. The enquiry should also encompass the causes of inequalities between both countries and individuals.

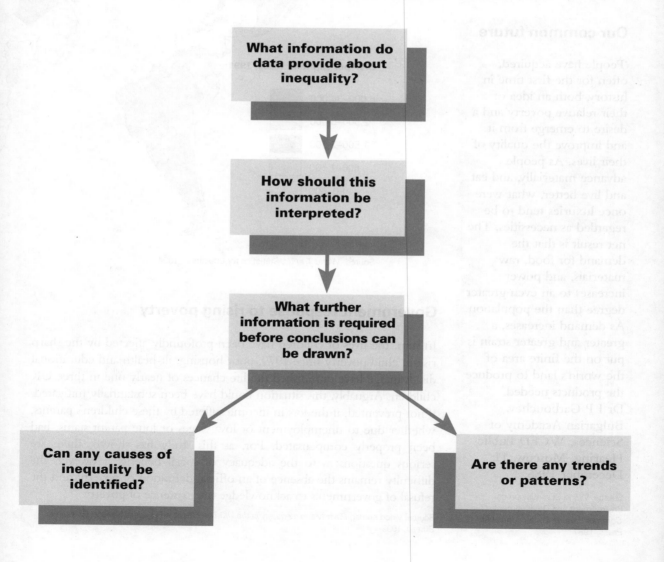

Opening evidence

Inequality in Tanzania

	% of GDP
Lowest 20%	2.4
2nd quintile	5.7
3rd quintile	10.4
4th quintile	18.7
Highest 20%	62.7

Source: World Bank, *World Development Report*, 1993

Our common future

'People have acquired, often for the first time in history, both an idea of their relative poverty and a desire to emerge from it and improve the quality of their lives. As people advance materially, and eat and live better, what were once luxuries tend to be regarded as necessities. The net result is that the demand for food, raw materials, and power increases to an even greater degree than the population. As demand increases, a greater and greater strain is put on the finite area of the world's land to produce the products needed.'
Dr I P Garbouchev, Bulgarian Academy of Sciences, WCED Public Hearing, Moscow, 11 December 1986

Source: World Commission on Environment and Development, *Our Common Future*, Oxford University Press, 1987

World income levels

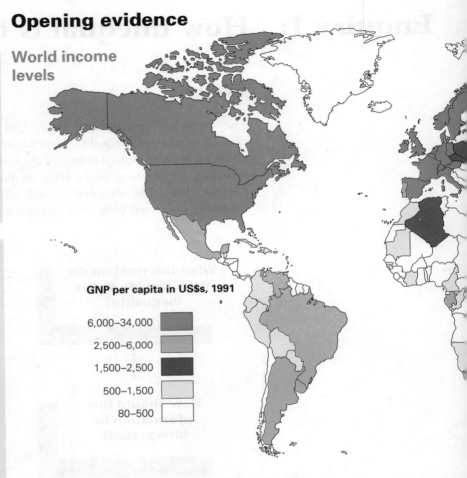

GNP per capita in US$s, 1991

6,000–34,000	
2,500–6,000	
1,500–2,500	
500–1,500	
80–500	

Source: *World Trends*, Statistics for Education, 1994

Government response to rising poverty

In sum, the lives of children have been profoundly affected by the sharp rise in child poverty since 1979: poor housing, ill–health and educational disadvantage have diminished the life chances of nearly one in three UK children. Arguably, this situation could have been substantially mitigated, if not prevented, if the loss in income suffered by these children's parents, whether due to unemployment or low wages or lone parent status, had been properly compensated. For, as this study has shown, there are serious questions as to the adequacy of social benefits. However, the difficulty remains the absence of an official definition of poverty, and the refusal of governments to acknowledge the existence of poverty.

Source: Vinod Kumar, *Poverty and Inequality in the UK: The Effects on Children*, National Children's Bureau, 1993

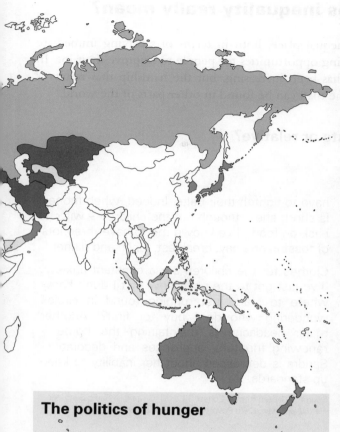

Is poverty just about money?

In a recent study of living standards during un-employment, 30 families were interviewed in depth and between them identified nine factors that had a bearing on their judgements of living standards:

- the amount of disposable *income* they had
- the items of *expenditure* they could or could not afford
- the level of *choice* or constraint that surrounded their pattern of expenditure
- the level of *financial security* that was felt
- the degree to which *expectations* were fulfilled
- the extent to which *self-esteem* could be upheld
- the feelings of *contentment* that surrounded life

Source: Jo Roll, *Understanding Poverty: A Guide to the Concepts and Measures,* Family Policy Study Centre, 1992

Equal members of society

The living conditions of most indigenous peoples stand in sharp contrast to the ideal proclaimed by the law. In addition, however, there is the notion, in most national legislation, that indigenous peoples are incapable of running their own affairs. This perception emerges most clearly in Brazil, where Indians live legally under a system of guardianship. The Civil Code of Brazil defines the Indian as incapable and under the guardianship of the Union whose delegated authority is the National Indian Foundation (FUNAI). The Indian is defined as a ward who must be led 'progressively and harmoniously towards integration with the wider society'. Emancipation is gained by the petitioner showing to a court that he or she speaks Portuguese, can make a useful contribution to society and understands the customs of the national community. To date no Amerindians have been emancipated.

Source: Julian Burger, *Report from the Frontier,* Zed Books, 1987

The politics of hunger

Hunger is not a modern malady. Hunger is, however, intolerable in the modern world in a way it could not have been in the past. This is not so much because it is more intense, but because widespread hunger is so unnecessary and unwarranted in the modern world. The enormous expansion of productive power that has taken place over the last few centuries has made it, perhaps for the first time, possible to guarantee adequate food for all, and it is in this context that the persistence of chronic hunger and the recurrence of virulent famines must be seen as being morally outrageous and politically unacceptable. If politics is 'the art of the possible', then conquering world hunger has become a political issue in a way it could not have been in the past.

Source: Jean Drèze and Amartya Sen, *Hunger and Public Action,* Clarendon Paperbacks, 1989

1 What does inequality really mean?

The world is an unequal place, both in terms of satisfying immediate needs and in providing opportunities for people to improve their lot. In the UK inequality has been increasing, but the hardship that results is generally less extreme than can be found in other parts of the world.

Poverty: absolute or relative?

On the breadline

Sandra receives benefits totalling £127.80 per week for herself and her three children. From this she pays £6.11 a week for council tax and water rates. Gas and electricity average about £5 each per week and she also pays £5 to a catalogue. She has no savings.

Sandra budgets meticulously each week, economising as much as possible and accounting for every penny. She tries to budget for lump sums too, buying Christmas presents from January onwards, saving up school clothing grants and 'robbing Peter to pay Paul' when bills come in. She pays fuel bills in several instalments, but to do this the whole family have to tighten their belts. Indeed, when money is short, she – though not the children – will cut back on food: 'I've known me to have three lots of toast in one day: breakfast, lunch and dinner.'

Clothes for the children are a constant anxiety: 'I've just got to the point now that I don't know where to start, just running round in circles wondering who do I buy for first?' Another major headache is maintaining the home – renewing furniture, appliances and decoration. Sandra is depressed about her inability to keep up standards.

Source: Adapted from R Cohen, J Coxall, G Craig, A Sadiq-Sangster, *Hardship Britain*, Child Poverty Action Group, 1992

Fight for survival

The community of Vertente, near the town of Alagoa Grande in Paraiba, Brazil, has always had it hard. Sixty families live there, squeezed onto five hectares of land. A black community, descendants of African slaves, they were already second class citizens. The 1990 drought brought them to the edge of death. Their banana trees were dry, fragile and cracking. Many had already fallen. The children were already pot-bellied from hunger, large lifeless eyes staring from faces so gaunt that they already appeared elderly. Many had ear and eye infections. One man was so hungry that he staggered as he walked, with his eyes out of focus as if he were drunk. In April 1990, no-one had been able to afford beans since January. Many people were able to eat only every few days.

Even in good years they only make just enough to feed themselves. There is nothing left over for clothes or medicines. The community has the highest level of child mortality in the region. They have survived until now on their bananas, their few animals, small plots of maize and manioc on rented land and casual labour on sugar plantations. They used to wait by the roadside for the trucks that came to hire day labourers. But now the trucks don't come. And now they don't have the energy to work. Even getting water is a major task. They have to go to the top of the hill to a spring which yields water drop by drop. It can take four hours to fill a pot.

Source: N MacDonald, *Brazil: A Mask Called Progress*, Oxfam, 1991

Poverty has been described as 'the inability to attain a minimal standard of living'. This fundamentally means not having enough to eat and is generally described as **absolute poverty**. In both examples above people were going without food, but in Brazil the state of affairs was obviously more extreme, as it had reached the point of being life threatening. The English family were enduring considerable hardship and were deprived of many things that we have come to accept as necessities, but were not suffering on the scale of the Brazilians. The two examples show the difference between absolute and **relative poverty**. Relative poverty can be defined as having sufficient income to meet basic physical needs, but insufficient to participate in society. (What full participation requires will vary from one society to another.) Sandra and her children come perilously close to slipping into absolute poverty as a diet of bread will not provide adequate nutrition. She is probably sacrificing her food in an attempt to maintain the family's participation in the customs and activities of life in the UK.

The existence of relative poverty implies some degree of inequality because 'participation in society' must be available to most members of society. It is, however, possible for a community to be in or near absolute poverty even if there is little or no inequality.

Within a range of countries inequality has different implications. The data in Figure 1.1 show how the UK and Brazil compare in terms of income distribution.

*Figure 1.1 **Income distribution***

% share of household income		
	Brazil	**UK**
Lowest 20%	2.1	7.9
Second quintile	4.9	12.4
Third quintile	8.9	17.0
Fourth quintile	16.8	22.7
Highest 20%	67.5	40.0

Source: World Bank, *World Development Report*, 1993; CSO, *Social Trends*, 1994

In total income terms, Brazil falls into the category of an upper middle-income country, but its distribution of income is so unequal that the poor are generally poorer than in many less developed countries.

Figure 1.2 World income distribution

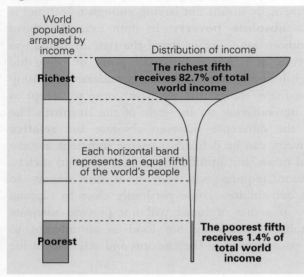

Source: *Human Development Report,*
UN Development Program,1992

On a world scale, the distribution of income is also very unequal. The richest fifth receives 82.7% of total world income and the poorest fifth receives 1.4% as Figure 1.2 shows.

2 Interpreting inequality

On any trip abroad, one of the first things you find out is how far the money goes. In Switzerland, the price of a cup of coffee provides an unpleasant surprise for someone travelling from the UK, whereas in Tunisia at least two cups can be bought for the same outlay. This implies that the cost of living can vary considerably between countries. Official data must therefore be looked at carefully if genuine comparisons are to be made.

In many publications, the GDP for each country is shown in US dollars. These figures are converted at the appropriate exchange rate to enable the reader to compare one country with another. In order to take the differing costs of living into account, a **purchasing power parity** (PPP) exchange rate will help to make the adjustment. It is calculated on the basis of the cost of a basket of goods in each country. If the same goods can be bought for £1 in the UK as can be bought for $1 in the USA, the purchasing power parity exchange rate should be £1 to $1, whatever the actual exchange rate between the currencies might be.

Figure 1.3 How far does the money go?

Country	GNP per capita ($)	Real GDP per capita (PPP$)
Canada	20,380	19,232
Singapore	11,200	15,880
Bahamas	11,550	11,235
Mexico	2,490	5,918
Malaysia	6,140	2,330
Philippines	2,303	730
India	360	1,072
Tanzania	110	572

Source: *Human Development Report*, UN Development Program,1993

The information in Figure 1.3 shows how much further money goes in some countries than in others. The first column shows GNP per capita, calculated on the basis of official exchange rates. The second column shows what happens to per capita GDP when purchasing power parity exchange rates are used. Some countries, such as Bahamas, scarcely change. This means that a dollar buys about the same amount in the Bahamas as it would in the USA. In others a dollar will buy much more.

Even the adjustment for purchasing power parity does not solve all the problems of comparison. The needs of people living in Tanzania are obviously different from the needs of those in Canada. Warm winter clothing and heating will be needed by Canadians and will, therefore, increase the cost of living. Dietary habits are also very different around the world, so a supply shortage that increases the price of a staple foodstuff will increase the cost of living but will not be reflected by purchasing power parities. It is difficult to select a basket of goods that can be used to make the comparison, because of these varied needs. Even within Europe, such comparisons can be misleading. In France, sliced bread is expensive and baguettes are cheap. In the UK, the reverse is the case. What type of bread should go into the basket? The lesson from this is that income data must be treated with caution, even when purchasing power parities are used.

3 The changing pattern

Figure 1.4 Ratio of income shares between richest and poorest of the world's population

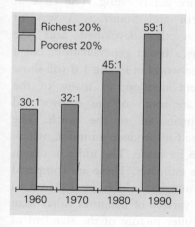

Source: *Human Development Report,* UN Development Program, 1992

The distribution of income among the world's population is growing increasingly unequal. Figure 1.4 shows the increasing pace of change. For every pound earned by the poorest 20%, the richest earned £30 in 1960. By 1990 the gap has widened to 59:1. In percentage terms, between 1960 and 1990, the share of global GNP of the countries with the richest 20% of world population increased from 70.2% to 82.7%. The poorest countries' share fell from 2.3% to 1.4%. From 1960 to 1970 the change was small, but it has increased in more recent years. Overall, in thirty years, the disparity has increased by almost 100%.

These figures disguise the true extent of inequality for two reasons. They are figures for economies, not individuals, so they hide the disparities within countries. The difference between the richest people in the richest country and the poorest people in the poorest country would be even more stark. Data on income distribution is only available from 41 countries, but even using this information it can be shown that the inequality ratio between the top and bottom of the range rises to 65:1. The second factor is that there is a higher representation of developed countries among those that provide data, so the real figures for inequality would show a greater disparity. The countries that do not provide data tend to be the poorest, where disparity is generally greater. It has been estimated that if all countries were taken into account, the ratio between the richest 20% and the poorest 20% could be 150:1.

These growing disparities are apparent not only when looking at income, but also in many other forms of economic activity.

Figure 1.5 Widening economic gaps

| | Percentage of global economic activity | | | |
| | Poorest 20% | | Richest 20% | |
	1960–70	1990	1960–70	1990
Global GNP	2.3	1.4	70.2	82.7
Trade	1.3	1.0	80.8	81.2
Commercial bank lending	0.3	0.2	72.3	94.6
Domestic investment	3.5	1.3	70.4	80.6
Domestic saving	3.5	1.0	70.4	80.5
Foreign private investment	3.4	2.7	73.3	58.4

Source: *Human Development Report*, UN Development Program, 1992

The data in Figure 1.5 show how economic activity is becoming increasingly concentrated in the developed and richer areas of the developing world. The growth of Japan, Malaysia and other Pacific Rim countries has changed the overall pattern, but has led to a concentration of investment in a small number of countries, including India and China, for example, but leaving others to fall behind.

Multiplier

Figure 1.6 The North and South

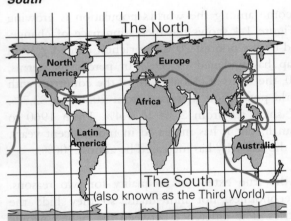

The North

North America   Europe

Africa

Latin America

Australia

The South
(also known as the Third World)

Source: *It's An Unfair World*, Oxfam, 1991

Absolute and relative value

As the poorest countries are growing less rapidly than the richest, there are further implications for their populations. In some fields of human development these poor countries are deteriorating. The table in Figure 1.7 uses North and South as a way of distinguishing between the developed and the developing world. It is a broad generalisation, but a glance at the map of the world in Figure 1.6 will show that it is a convenient division, as many of the developing countries are south of the equator and many developed countries fall to the north. The South–North gap is used to produce an index, which enables comparisons to be made. The index is drawn from a set of national, regional and other estimates. These are compared with the average for all industrialised countries, which are indexed to equal 100. In constructing this index, a variety of measures other than income are used in order to provide a fuller picture of the standard of living in a country. Both Figures 1.7 and 1.8 use such measures to demonstrate the relative positions of the developed and developing world. The column labelled 'Absolute disparity' shows that, although the South is improving, the North is improving faster. In 1960, the gap between the percentage of the population in tertiary education in the North and South was 15%. By 1990 the gap had risen to 29%.

Source: Mark Bryant (ed.), *Turn Over a New Leaf*, Earthscan, 1990

Figure 1.7 Widening disparity in human progress

	North		South		Absolute disparity	
	1960	1990	1960	1990	1960	1990
Mean years of schooling	9	10	3.5	3.7	5.5	6.3
Tertiary education %	18	37	3	8	15	29
Scientists and technicians per 1,000 population	51	81	6	9	45	72
Expenditure on R&D $bn	196	434	13	18	183	416
Telephones per 1,000 people	130	436	9	26	121	440
Radios per 1,000 people	449	1,008	32	173	417	835

Source: *Human Development Report*, UN Development Program, 1992

Figure 1.8 Narrowing disparity in human progress

	North		South		Absolute disparity	
	1960	1990	1960	1990	1960	1990
Life expectancy (years)	69	74.5	46.2	62.8	22.8	11.7
Adult literacy %	95	97	46	64	49	33
Nutrition (% of requirement)	124	134	90	109	34	25
Infant mortality per 1,000	37	13	150	74	123	61
Child mortality per 1,000	46	18	233	112	187	94
Access to safe water	100	100	40	68	60	32

Source: *Human Development Report*, UN Development Program, 1992

The implication of the information in Figure 1.7 is serious because although both groups show some progress, the pace in the countries of the developing world is very slow when compared with that of those in the developed world. The South is still tending to fall behind the North. This means that many developing countries are unattractive as locations for investment. Their lack of social and economic infrastructure has a negative effect on their international competitiveness.

In some of the more fundamental aspects of life, however, there is a pattern of improvement. Figure 1.8 shows the areas in which the gap is narrowing.

There has been significant improvement in health and nutrition in much of the developing world. However, these are average figures for developed and developing countries, so there are still many in which the standard of living is very low.

The widening gap is not just an international feature. Within the UK, the gap between the rich and the poor has widened in the last 15 years. Figure 1.9 shows how different groups in society have gained and lost in relation to others. In every category, the poorest 10%, despite having gained in absolute terms, are relatively worse off when compared with their more affluent counterparts. Single women show a high percentage change in real income, but in absolute terms they have not yet reached comparability with their male equivalents. This reflects the world pattern of improvement for everyone, but with the better off gaining more, more quickly.

Figure 1.9 Real weekly earnings

Earnings after deductions*	£ and %			% change	
	1971	1981	1991	1971 –81	1981 –91
Single man					
Lowest decile point	94.9	103.6	125.5	9.2	21.2
Median	104.3	153.7	202.6	9.5	31.8
Highest decile point	221.9	250.3	365.2	12.8	45.9
Single woman					
Lowest decile point	60.8	77.3	99.2	27.1	28.3
Median	84.9	106.8	148.6	25.8	39.1
Highest decile point	132.4	173.2	252.7	30.8	45.8
Married man, no children					
Lowest decile point	101.8	111.6	133.8	9.6	19.9
Median	147.2	161.7	210.9	9.8	30.5
Highest decile point	228.8	258.3	373.5	12.9	44.6
Married man, 2 children					
Lowest decile point					
Family credit claimed	119.1	129.3	157.6	8.5	12.9
Family credit not claimed	119.1	129.3	149.9	8.5	16.0
Median	164.5	179.4	227.0	9.0	26.6
Highest decile point	246.2	276.0	389.6	12.1	41.2

★ *After deduction of income tax, national insurance, child benefit and family credit.*

Source: CSO, *Social Trends*, 1993

Comparing inequality

Two useful techniques for making comparisons between the degree of inequality within and between countries are the Lorenz curve and the Gini co-efficient, which can be drawn from it.

The Lorenz curve shows how unequal distribution is by the areas between the diagonal line and the curve. The greater the area, the greater is the inequality. Figure 1.10 shows how it works. Along the horizontal axis the numbers refer to the cumulative, proportion of total population. So 10 represents the bottom 10% of the population and 40 includes the bottom 40%. By the time 100 is reached, all the population has been included. The vertical axis is also cumulative, and shows the proportion of income received by every percentage of the population.

Figure 1.10 A Lorenz curve

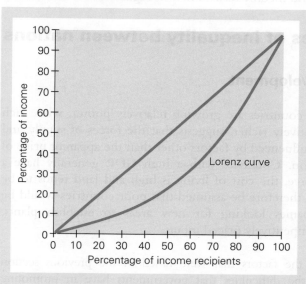

Figure 1.11 Income distribution

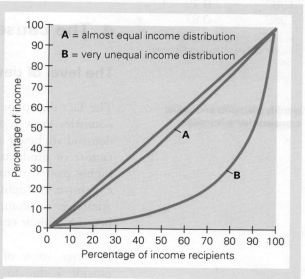

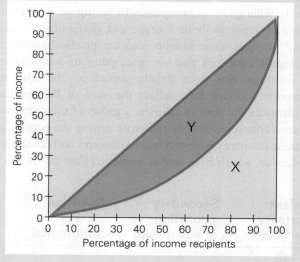

Figure 1.12 Calculating a Gini co-efficient

The curve can be plotted using, for example, the quintile data for the UK and Brazil in Figure 1.1 By drawing a curve for each country, a comparison can be made of the distribution of income. Along the diagonal line, the percentage of income received is always equal to the percentage of population, so distribution is perfectly equal. A curve such as A in Figure 1.11 is very close to equality, whereas the one labelled B represents a very unequal distribution. Comparisons can also be made of one country over a period of time by plotting the quintile distribution for each year.

To calculate the Gini co-efficient, the ratio of the area between the diagonal and the curve (the shaded area labelled Y in Figure 1.12) and the triangle in which it lies is calculated.

The co-efficient is therefore worked out by dividing area Y by X+Y or:

$$\frac{Y}{X+Y}$$

Figure 1.13 Global income disparity 1960–1989

Year	Gini co-efficient
1960	0.69
1970	0.71
1980	0.79
1989	0.87

Source: *Human Development Report*, UN Development Program, 1992

Supply, demand and price; comparative advantage

A result of 0 would mean that distribution was perfectly equal, whereas 1 would mean perfect inequality. The two ends of the spectrum, of course, never occur. If the result falls between 0.2 and 0.35, a country has a relatively equal distribution of income. Between 0.5 and 0.7, it becomes highly inequitable, as is demonstrated by the progressively higher ratios for world income distribution in Figure 1.13.

4 The causes of inequality between nations

The level of development

The fact that poor countries are growing relatively poorer, while rich countries grow relatively richer, suggests that the forces of supply and demand are being influenced by factors other than the apparent price of factors of production. Countries with a high GDP, generally have a highly paid workforce, the cost of living is high and land tends to be expensive. It might therefore be assumed that poor countries would be attractive to companies looking for new areas to establish plants, because of their competitively priced inputs.

However, some of the factors that were raised in the previous section provide a clue to the difficulties that governments have in promoting development and the unwillingness of companies to set up or expand in such countries. (This can apply to both foreign and domestically based companies.) Figure 1.7 provides some insights into the practical problems encountered by developing countries that are attempting to industrialise. These data include countries that have already started on the road to development and therefore do not fully reflect the way of life for the poorest. Figure 1.14 identifies the state of affairs in a group of the countries classified as 'low income economies' and are therefore among the poorest in the world. (Some of these countries have also had to contend with civil wars and other political upheavals, which have further worsened their positions.)

Figure 1.14 Indicators from low income economies

	Life expectancy (years)	Adult literacy (%)	Infant mortality (per 1,000)	Secondary education (% of age group)	Nutrition (% of requirements)
Mozambique	47	67	149	7	70
Chad	47	70	124	7	74
Sierra Leone	42	79	145	16	79
Bangladesh	51	65	103	17	83
Burkino Faso	48	82	133	7	83
Nigeria	52	49	85	20	85

Source: World Bank, *World Development Report*, 1993; *Human Development Report*, UN Development Program, 1993

Investment, human capital, productivity and costs of production

The low levels of education and health make rapid development an unlikely prospect. Low levels of investment in human capital result in low levels of labour productivity. A workforce may be cheap, but if its members do not have the necessary level of education or physical health to cope with the work or training there is little incentive to induce a company to move in. The provision of roads, railways and other forms of infrastructure are equally undeveloped, and therefore it would be difficult to attract industry. The political instability of some of these countries has also contributed to their lack of appeal.

All these factors would, of course, add to costs for any firm considering investment in these extremely poor countries. Not only would the shortcomings of the location increase costs but also the provision for expatriate workers would add to the total. Supply and demand, therefore, works after all.

Trade

Developing countries have, traditionally been the producers of primary products (i.e. agricultural products, minerals and fuels). Apart from the periods of both world wars, there has been a tendency for the price of such commodities to fall relative to manufactured goods. This took on a new dimension in the 1980s when prices of some products fell by almost 50%. Tea and coffee, for example, fell to prices which were equivalent, in real terms, to pre-war levels. Some countries, which depend heavily on one or two primary products, have therefore had to face a serious shortfall in their export earnings.

Not only have prices fallen but throughout the twentieth century, they have also fluctuated erratically. Primary products have always tended to suffer price variations, because they are so subject to changes in supply caused by the weather and other factors that are difficult to control. In the case of glut, producer countries are often desperate to sell their output, as they need foreign currency and so cannot wait until a better price can be obtained. Economic and political factors can also affect prices. Recessions in the industrialised world have led to a fall in demand for raw materials. The changes in Eastern Europe and Russia during the early 1990s caused increased demand for some commodities, while increasing the supply of others. The prices of grain and meat, for example, were kept high because of the former Soviet Union's inability to maintain food supplies, but in order to earn foreign currency they sold more bauxite and copper. This had an adverse effect on the prices that Ghana and Zambia could obtain for their exports.

Price elasticity of demand

Income elasticity of demand

Elasticity of supply

Over the years there has also been a world-wide tendency for supply to increase in general because production has become more efficient and new countries have entered the market, despite the trend of falling prices.

The second unfortunate trend for primary producers has been the fall in demand. This has been caused by the development of substitutes such as glass fibre, which replaces copper wire in the telecommunications industry. Synthetic fibres have replaced cotton and linen, and plastics have been substituted for rubber and some metals.

As exporters of primary products and importers of manufactured goods, such countries will suffer when the price of primary products falls in relation to the price of manufactures. The relationship between the price of imports and exports is known as the **terms of trade**. The following formula shows how the index of the terms of trade can be calculated. The indices are calculated using weighted averages of a wide range of imports and exports.

$$\text{Index of terms of trade} = \frac{\text{Index of export prices}}{\text{Index of import prices}}$$

The trends described above have badly affected the **terms of trade** of many developing countries. In Figure 1.15 both the trend and fluctuations can be seen. The Second World War boosted their relative value, but by the late 1980s they had fallen back to pre-war levels. The evidence suggests some decline even when allowance is made for the improvement in quality of manufactured imports.

Tariffs and quotas

Trade restrictions have a significant effect on the GNP of developing countries. It has been estimated by the World Bank that these countries lose $75 billion worth of trade every year because of such barriers. This is equivalent to 3% of GNP. The causes and implications will be discussed in Enquiry 3.

Figure 1.15 The terms of trade for primary products

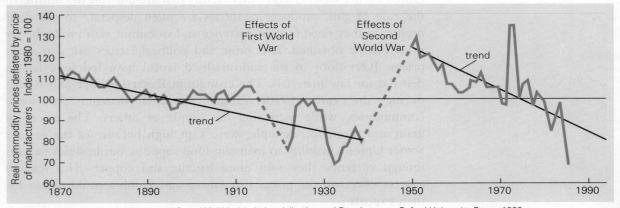

Source: Tom Hewitt, Hazel Johnson and Dave Wield (eds), *Industrialisation and Development*, Oxford University Press, 1992

Labour

Emigration has both a positive and a negative impact on a developing country. The positive effect is that migrants send money home to their families and this can make a significant contribution to a country's GNP. The remittances are often made in the host country's currency and therefore add to the recipient country's pool of foreign exchange. Figure 1.16 shows the impact that remittances can have. In Egypt, they are equivalent to 57% of the export bill and therefore ease the burden of payments in foreign currency as well as forming a significant injection into the country's economy. The multiplier effect of remittances to Egypt has been calculated as 2.2, so every $1,000 that is returned to the country increases GNP by $2,200.

Figure 1.16 Money sent home by migrants

Country	Remittances $bn	As % of GNP	As % of exports	As % of imports
Egypt	4.3	13.3	166	57
Portugal	3.4	7.5	26	18
Turkey	3.0	4.1	26	19
India	2.7	0.9	17	14
Pakistan	1.9	4.7	41	27
Morocco	1.3	6.0	40	24
Bangladesh	0.8	3.9	59	22
Jordan	0.6	10.6	61	27
Tunisia	0.5	4.8	16	11
Colombia	0.5	1.2	8	9
Philippines	0.4	0.8	5	3

Source: *Human Development Report*, UN Development Program, 1992

The drawback to emigration is that it is usually the skilled workers who leave. It is very tempting for highly trained personnel to leave a country where pay is low and opportunities few, when the industrialised countries can offer them far more. Some countries produce a surplus of graduates because their systems are copied from developed countries, where there is a greater requirement. Somalia, for example, educates five times as many graduates as it can employ. Most of Africa, however, suffers from shortages, and migration accentuates the problem. Sudan lost 17% of its doctors and dentists, 20% of university teachers, 30% of engineers and 45% of surveyors in one year. Not only do such movements deprive a country of skilled practitioners, but they also remove the scope for training the next generation, so the impact can be long lasting. Both creating surplus graduates and migration impose a cost if the state has paid for their education.

The developed world has tightened immigration controls. The total number of migrants has often not been reduced, but the developed world has become increasingly unwilling to accept people who do not have skills for which there is a demand. This has two negative effects on the economies of developing countries. First, by restricting immigration to skilled workers, the people who are most needed by their country of origin are removed and the structure of the labour force becomes more heavily weighted towards the lower skilled. Secondly, the families of those with skills are more likely to be able to support themselves, so the level of remittances will be lower.

Foreign investment

It is sometimes claimed that foreign direct investment (FDI) in developing countries is a high proportion of the total. This is, however, very misleading:

- In 1980 25% of FDI went to the developing world, while in 1990 17% of FDI went to the developing world.
- Transnational corporations employ less than 1% of the economically active population of developing countries.
- Most FDI is concentrated in relatively few developing countries. 74% went to 10 countries in 1990.

The relationship between the average for the 1980s and the figures for 1991, as shown in Figure 1.17, illustrates the trends in each country. The Pacific Rim features significantly in those in which inward investment is growing. Investment in Latin America is tending to fall, while in sub-Saharan Africa there is little change.

Figure 1.17 The ten largest recipients of foreign direct investment in the South

	% of FDI going to developing world 1980–89	Net FDI 1991 ($m)
Brazil	12	1,600
Singapore	12	n.a.
Mexico	11	4,762
China	10	4,366
Hong Kong	7	n.a.
Malaysia	6	3,455
Egypt	6	253
Argentina	4	2,439
Thailand	3	2,014
Colombia	3	420

Source: *Human Development Report*, UN Development Program, 1992, World Bank, *World Development Report*, 1993

A brief glance would suggest that countries that had very low costs, such as those of sub-Saharan Africa, would be attractive to industry, but on further investigation it appears that cheap factors of production do not always lead to a high rate of return on investment. In G7 countries the rate of return on foreign direct investment has averaged 16.5% between 1987 and 1990, whereas in sub-Saharan Africa it was 6.6%. This can be attributed to a variety of causes. The least developed countries tend to have a poorer level of infrastructure, which slows down the process of producing goods and services and therefore generates additional cost. The labour force tends to be less productive because of lower levels of education and training. The lack of political stability creates uncertainty and often leads to higher borrowing charges and exchange controls, which again raise costs. Interest rates in developing countries are frequently four times as high as those of developed countries. This may not deter foreign direct investment, as multinationals can usually borrow on world capital markets, but it will have a negative effect on local companies, which develop to provide goods and services to them. In many cases, these factors outweigh the benefits that are gained by establishing factories in what are thought of as low-cost locations.

There is also a spiral effect at work, because the home market in a developing country may be important to companies considering an investment project. The richer the country, the more attractive it will, therefore, be.

5 The causes of inequality between individuals

The ownership of wealth

Wealth and income are different. Income is a return to factors of production. People work, earning income in return. They lend their cash assets in return for interest payments, or sometimes they buy shares (or property) and receive dividend payments (or rent). All these payments are classified as income. A person's wealth, on the other hand, consists of their actual assets: cash, property, shares, bank deposits and so on. In all countries wealth is unequally distributed, and this is a major aspect of inequality generally.

In the UK 50% of the wealth is held by 10% of the population. This is adjusted when wealth is more broadly interpreted. Figure 1.18 on page 18 shows how the addition of pension rights spreads ownership considerably. As wealth is an important factor in determining future living standards, pension rights can justifiably be included.

Wealth Distribution could also be used within the essay question.

Figure 1.18 Distribution of wealth

Most wealthy	% of marketable wealth owned	% of marketable wealth plus occupational and state pension rights★
1%	18	11
5%	37	26
10%	51	37
25%	72	60
50%	93	84

★ Latest valuation.

Source: CSO, *Social Trends*, 1993

Much wealth is accumulated through the earnings of capital rather than labour. It is often kept in the same family through inheritance. The tax system sets out to redistribute wealth on death, but with careful planning, much of this can be avoided. The government regarded such taxes as a disincentive to set up in business, since they made it difficult to keep the business in the family, so during the 1980s, it was made easier to pass money and possessions from one generation to the next. As wealth generates income, it has a significant effect on the standard of living of those who have more of it.

Supply and demand

Differentials in earnings between individuals relate to the demand for and supply of the skills they possess. With a skill that is in short supply in an industry where demand for the end product is high, rewards will be high. On the other hand, those trained in skills that have become redundant will find it difficult to earn a living unless they retrain.

Structural change

This is exemplified by the changing patterns in the UK economy, where the decline of heavy industry has led to a fall in demand for people with particular specialist skills. As a result, the regions associated with coal, steel and shipbuilding became depressed. Manufacturing industries, in general, were affected by the recession of the early 1980s, thus widening the areas affected by a lack of demand for labour.

During this period, service industries had been growing and wages had risen in that sector. As much of this growth took place in the South East, it increased the regional imbalance that already existed. The recession of the early 1990s, however, hit the service industries particularly hard and had a smaller impact on manufacturing. The pattern of demand and supply in the labour market is very sensitive to such fluctuations.

On a smaller scale, demand for labour with a particular skill can disappear overnight, when new technology enables machines to replace people. Equally, technology that increases individuals' productivity should increase their value as employees.

The supply of labour for some occupations is much more flexible than for others. The elasticity of supply often relates to the degree of training that is required. The longer the training period, the more inelastic supply will be. It takes many years to increase the supply of doctors, for example, but a much shorter period to produce more car assembly workers.

Throughout the developed world in recent years there has been a significant fall in the number of unskilled jobs. This is partly the result of shifts in comparative advantage: many of the unskilled jobs are now being done in the developing countries, which have been able to industrialise successfully. Partly also, it is because of new technologies, which have mechanised much unskilled work. The end result of this has been that unskilled people in developed countries have experienced very high rates of unemployment. Those in work have found that with the demand for their services reduced, wage rates have fallen relative to those of skilled people. Both trends have increased inequality in the developed countries. In effect, there is an almost infinitely elastic supply of unskilled people. The increased education and training effort needed to deal with this problem cannot be expected to bring about a speedy adjustment.

A wide variety of factors affect an individual's role in the labour market. Some, such as the extent of training, will, justifiably in terms of the market, influence how much they earn. Others, such as age, sex and race lead to discrimination, which can reduce potential earning power.

Figure 1.19 Typical occupations in each decile range of the distribution of gross weekly earnings

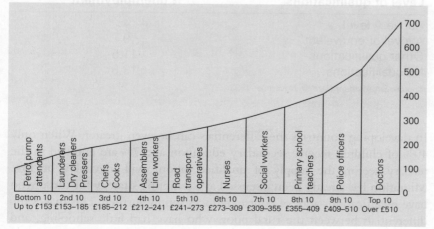

Bottom 10 — Petrol pump attendants — Up to £153
2nd 10 — Launderers Dry cleaners Pressers — £153–185
3rd 10 — Chefs Cooks — £185–212
4th 10 — Assemblers Line workers — £212–241
5th 10 — Road transport operatives — £241–273
6th 10 — Nurses — £273–309
7th 10 — Social workers — £309–355
8th 10 — Primary school teachers — £355–409
9th 10 — Police officers — £409–510
Top 10 — Doctors — Over £510

Source: *Employment Gazette*, November 1993

Qualifications

Figure 1.19 gives a general impression of the relationship between qualifications and earnings. Those at the upper end of the distribution tend to need more qualifications than those who earn less. The distribution graph in Figure 1.20 on page 20 helps to explain why police officers, primary school teachers and social workers are in the upper deciles. The bulk of employees earn between £150 and £400 per week and very few earn over this amount, so the top decile contains all those who earn above £510, which is relatively low in terms of the total spread of income.

Figure 1.20 Distribution of gross weekly earnings

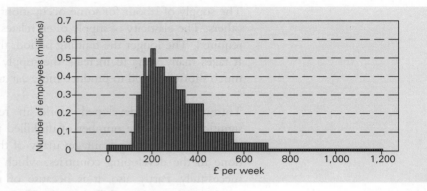

Source: *Employment Gazette,* November 1993

One other factor is significant in explaining earnings differentials: employees in the upper–income ranges are more likely to be members of trade unions or professional bodies. This means that they have greater bargaining power in pay negotiations.

Figure 1.21 looks at the other side of the coin. Earning power is not only related to wages of those in work, but also depends on the ability to find a job. People with higher levels of qualification are less likely to be unemployed. The data show how the risk of unemployment rises as the level of qualifications falls. Once unemployed, an individual typically falls into the lowest decile of income received.

Figure 1.21 Qualifications and unemployment

Level of qualifications	% unemployment
Above A level	4
A level or equivalent	9
Other qualifications	11.5
No qualifications	13.5

Source: *Employment Gazette,* November 1993

In developing countries the differentials can be even greater. When only 40% of children receive secondary education and 7% are enrolled in the tertiary sector, the supply of qualified labour will inevitably be low. Migration has already been discussed as a tempting strategy for those who have qualifications and, of course, reduces supply further. This makes the differentials between the rural poor, who have had little schooling, and the urban middle classes even greater than in the developed world.

Discrimination

An age old problem

AGE Concern launched a campaign to fight prejudice against old people, backed by posters that featured 'old codger' John Fisher, a 70-year-old from London and others of a woman labelled 'silly old moo'.

The posters will go up on sites across Britain with the slogan: 'How long before people call you names? Fight ageism now'. The photographs were taken by David Bailey, who is 55. He said: 'Ageism is a big problem and will affect you and me. When you are old you are expected to be serene and wise but at the same time you are dismissed, patronised and called names.'

Age Concern is lobbying for legislation against age discrimination, similar to that for racism and sexism. It said that the stereotype of an elderly person was

someone in poor health who lived in poverty and had lost all interest in sex. In reality, only 3% of people over 65 lived in institutions and only 22% of those over 55 said their health was bad.

Newspaper articles about hang-gliding grandmothers and elderly people being conned or attacked were patronising and reinforced the stereotypes, the charity added. Older people also suffered prejudice in the job market, with many being forced to take early retirement, irrespective of ability.

'Those caught in the unemployment trap after the age of 45 are likely to suffer the consequences for the rest of their lives, in terms of finances and lost self esteem,' Age Concern said.

Source: *The Times*, 16 January 1993

Figure 1.22 Average gross weekly earnings by age-group

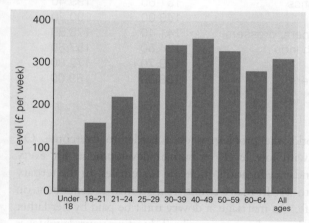

Source: *Employment Gazette*, November 1993

Age is one factor for which there is no legal protection in the employment market. The article above suggests that there should be and the data reinforce the view. The statistics for pay in Figure 1.22 show that after the age of 50 income declines. This picture is composite, because earnings rise with experience and decline as human capital declines. The middle group may be expected to do more overtime to support their families. There is evidence, however, that firms are less willing to employ people as they grow older. Figure 1.23 on page 22 reflects the fact that the young and the old are both more likely to be made redundant.

Despite the fact that sexism and racism are both controlled by legislation, inequalities still appear. Not all of them are as a result of deliberate attempts to treat people differently, but some do relate to attitudes that are hard to change. Women's hourly pay rate is still substantially lower than that received by men, as shown in Figure 1.24 on page 22. Because women may give up paid employment while having children, they are often lower down pay scales than men of equivalent age. Also, the fields in which women are concentrated, such as catering and clerical work, tend to be low paid. In some occupations attempts are made to overcome these factors, but the state of the labour market has an effect on the employers' desires for change. In the late

Demand and supply

Figure 1.23 Age and redundancy

Age	Spring 1992	Summer 1992	Autumn 1992	Winter 1992	Spring 1993
16–24	18.6	17.9	17.8	27.6	16.6
25–34	14.2	11.5	14.3	15.3	11.4
35–44	12.8	12.3	10.9	13.6	10.1
45–54	14.3	11.8	14.1	15.5	10.5
55+	17.7	16.2	17.3	17.8	16.5

Source: *Employment Gazette*, January 1994

1980s it was thought that the demographic trends of an ageing population would make the retention of women in employment an attractive proposition. Companies started to make plans for crèches and other schemes that would encourage women to continue working when they had children. However, the recession which followed created a pool of surplus labour so these expensive plans were often dropped.

Figure 1.24 Male–female differentials

	(£)	
	Women	Men
Cleaners and domestics	151.60	199.40
Sales assistants	149.00	190.20
Launderers, dry cleaners, pressers	141.40	178.80
Kitchen porters and hands	134.50	157.80
Bar staff	129.70	172.80
Waitresses and waiters	138.30	169.00

Source: *New Earnings Survey*, 1992

In the developing world, the problem is even harder to overcome. On average, in countries with low levels of human development, for every hundred males in secondary education, there are 62 females. In the tertiary sector, the figure falls to 41. In many countries a woman is dependent on men throughout her life. On marriage, a dowry must be paid by her father so that she is not a burden on her new family. 'Educating your daughter is like watering another man's field' is a traditional Bengali saying, which explains why the problem exists. Despite the fact that dowries are illegal in Bangladesh, the practice still continues and women's status remains unchanged. Until education is available to both sexes equally, it will be difficult for these countries to make full use of this valuable resource.

The sources of inequality that have been discussed here are caused by many factors, including social attitudes and government policy. If change is desired, it cannot be achieved overnight and in any event, some countries or groups of countries may feel that it is in their interest to maintain a degree of inequality. These issues will be discussed in later Enquiries.

Open Question

Why might countries wish to maintain a degree of inequality?

Enquiry 2:   Can aid reduce inequality?

Scope

Aid is ostensibly given in order to assist countries in the improvement of economic and social conditions. It reaches its destination through many different channels. This enquiry looks at the effectiveness of different kinds of aid in achieving the fundamental objective, and how its impact has varied in different countries over the years. The motives of both donors and recipients are questioned and the issue of dependency is explored.

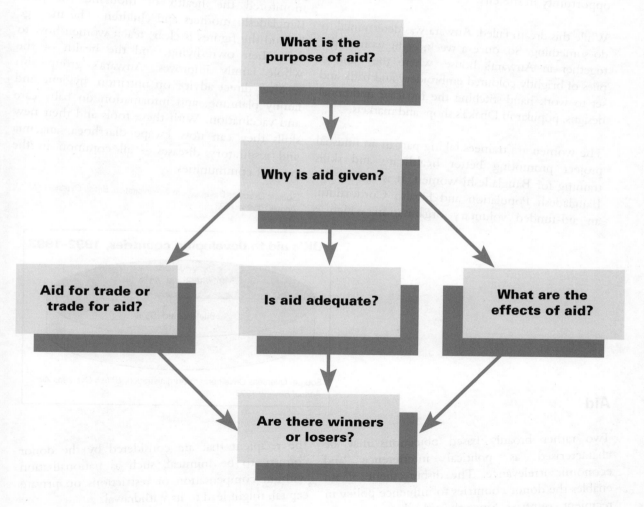

What is the purpose of aid?

Why is aid given?

Aid for trade or trade for aid?

Is aid adequate?

What are the effects of aid?

Are there winners or losers?

Opening evidence

A stitch in time

Anwara is 19, her husband has left her for another woman and she is bringing up a baby on her own in a broken-down one-room house with no water or power. Originally from a tiny rural community 60 kilometres south of Dhaka, Anwara and her husband were just one of thousands of couples leaving a hard life on the land for what they thought was money and opportunity in the city.

While this dream failed, Anwara was determined to do something. So, once a week, eight women get together in Anwara's house, where they unload piles of brightly coloured embroidery and batik and set to work hand-stitching the intricate traditional designs, popular in Dhaka's shops and markets.

The women are trainees taking part in an unusual project promoting better healthcare and skills training for Bangladeshi women. It is run by the Bangladesh Population and Health Consortium, an aid-funded voluntary organisation which is based in Dhaka, but operates similar schemes all over the country.

The women are learning skills that will feed them and their children and help pay the rent. But the project means much more than that. In poor areas like the Dhaka slums, good health and good skills go hand in hand. Since this project began four-and-a-half years ago, BPHC has monitored the health of thousands of poor Bangladeshi mothers and children. The message behind the figures is clear: teach women how to earn their own living, and the health of the whole family improves. Anwara's group also receives direct advice on nutrition, hygiene and family planning, and information on baby care and vaccination. With these tools and their new skills they can now escape diarrhoea, anaemia and respiratory diseases – all common in the poorest communities.

Source: Overseas Development Administration, *British Overseas Aid: Annual Review 1993*

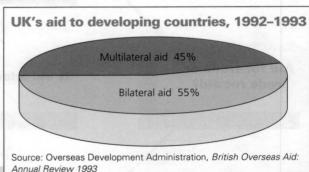

UK's aid to developing countries, 1992–1993

Multilateral aid 45%

Bilateral aid 55%

Source: Overseas Development Administration, *British Overseas Aid: Annual Review 1993*

Aid

Two rather broadly based objections may be characterised as political interference and economic irrelevance. The disbursement of aid enables the donor countries to influence policy in recipient countries. Since the aid is being given to encourage development, activities on the part of the recipient that are considered by the donor country to be inimical, such as nationalisation without compensation or restrictions on private capital, might lead to its withdrawal.

Source: Alan B Mountjoy (ed.), *The Third World: Problems and Perspectives*, Macmillan, 1978

Nurses fly out to help Angolans

While peace talks were taking place in neighbouring Zambia, four UK government-funded emergency aid flights reached Angola carrying emergency relief supplies. The consignments of non-food aid, part of Britain's £10 million emergency aid package to war-torn Angola, were delivered to the United Nations Children's Fund (UNICEF) in November to help implement the accelerated programme of mass immunisation currently under way.

Between 40 and 55 per cent of Angola's infant mortality is caused by measles and diarrhoeal disease. Ten British nurses recruited by the Overseas Development Administration through International Health Exchange accompanied the second relief flight. They aimed to immunise 70,000 children under the age of five and 950,000 mothers in 30 days.

Source: *British Overseas Development Newspaper*, January 1994

Help to the world

THE biggest Third World buyers of British arms since 1980 all obtained large amounts of British aid. Countries such as Indonesia, Malaysia, and Pakistan all showed hefty leaps in their aid allocations (196.4%, 99% and 55% respectively) – yet they also found the cash to buy aircraft, weapons and ammunition.

But, as well as the arms companies and the governments of countries that were neither the poorest nor the most humanitarian, there was a third, so far overlooked, beneficiary of Britain's overseas-aid budget.

Inquiries reveal that, for years, a handful of companies took the bulk of the Overseas Development Administration's Aid and Trade Provision (ATP) – intended 'to help British companies to win sound investment projects in developing countries where there is a reasonable prospect of follow-up business on commercial terms', in the words of the Overseas Development Administration. Because of its links to future trade, ATP is administered jointly by the Overseas Development Administration and the Department of Trade and Industry.

Source: *Independent on Sunday*, 13 February 1994

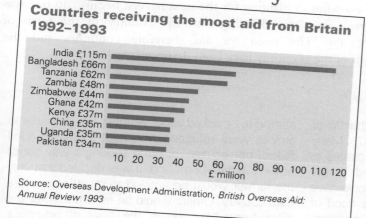

Countries receiving the most aid from Britain 1992–1993

India £115m
Bangladesh £66m
Tanzania £62m
Zambia £48m
Zimbabwe £44m
Ghana £42m
Kenya £37m
China £35m
Uganda £35m
Pakistan £34m

10 20 30 40 50 60 70 80 90 100 110 120
£ million

Source: Overseas Development Administration, *British Overseas Aid: Annual Review 1993*

'It's only some foreign aid mission members, sir. I told them we wanted to be self-reliant and didn't want to depend on any country and sent them away!'

1 What is aid?

Bangladesh: the need for instant relief

Flooding is normal in Bangladesh. At monsoon time a third of the land (22 million hectares) is usually under water. Farmers depend on this for the successful harvest of their rice and jute. But when flood waters are abnormally high it can spell catastrophe.

When a vicious cyclone hit the south-east coast in April 1991, 200,000 people died and 4 million were made homeless. More than a dozen islands in the Bay of Bengal were swamped by tidal waves. Particularly hard-hit were communities living on the southern-most islands, some of which were little more than large sand bars.

Oxfam staff were among the first to visit the area to assess relief needs. Food, clean water and temporary shelter were identified as the most urgently needed items. Within 24 hours of the cyclone, local staff had started relief distribution on Hatiya Island.

Links with an efficiently run local organisation made this quick response possible. Food was purchased locally instead of being shipped in from the mainland and a damage assessment survey was carried out to determine which landless families were most in need of emergency supplies.

Source: Oxfam and Bangladesh

The world is frequently called upon to help countries with relief for disasters, both man–made and natural. The aid which was provided to help flood victims in Bangladesh was **emergency aid**. This is humanitarian rather than development aid. The poorest countries, of course, have the greatest difficulties in repairing the damage that has been caused because their resources are very limited. This aid is for consumption – short-term help to overcome immediate problems of shortages of food and shelter. Such help must not be continued for too long, because the maintenance of the local market is essential for the recovery of the economy. There have been cases where local farmers could see no point in planting for the next harvest because no one was buying grain as it was flooding into the country in the form of emergency aid. The need for aid therefore continues and the foundations of the economy have been destroyed.

Resettling the boat people

The exodus from Vietnam began after the fall of the South Vietnamese government in 1975. Many fled in leaky boats, braving storms and pirates in the South China Seas. Thousands died in the escape. Over the years, 700,000 boat people have been resettled, mainly in the West. The flood of people continued and many spent years in prison-like camps in Hong Kong and Malaysia. Questions

started to be asked about whether the Vietnamese arrivals were refugees who had 'a well founded fear of persecution' or were seeking a way out of poverty in their homeland. It was decided that only the former would be entitled to resettlement in a third country. Others would be returned. After the initial furore died down the flow of returnees increased steadily.

Vietnamese boat people.

For those who have returned, there are ample opportunities to start a new life. Skills training and development projects are provided under programmes by the United Nations High Commission for Refugees (UNHCR) using funds from countries which support the Comprehensive Plan of Action (CPA), which has been established to cope with the repatriation.

The European Union has a £130 million reintegration programme available to the Vietnamese, including the returnees. 'We don't want to create a special class of people. We try to spread the benefits of our programme,' said the Regional Director of the European Community International Programme. 'We want the returnees to be successful, but we are not obligated to make their dreams happen. They have to do it on their own.'

Unaccompanied minors have always caused concern. Tran Thanh Hung, who is 17, left Vietnam with a group of friends in 1989 and ended up in Indonesia. After three and a half years in a camp, he concluded that he would never be resettled and decided to return, before his case was resolved. He is now back with his family, learning to be a mechanic at a vocational training centre.

The EU International Programme also lends money to help people rebuild their lives. Le Long Tien, who spent six months in a refugee camp in Malaysia, has used two successive loans to assist the development of a thriving noodle restaurant, which he runs with his family. He also received $410 repatriation allowance, which is equivalent to slightly more than the annual salary of a government employee. The CPA ceased offering this to returners because they found that it was encouraging people to leave Vietnam a second time, following their repatriation.

Official Development Assistance (ODA) may be given to enable areas to become self-sufficient. The example from Vietnam demonstrates how aid given co-operatively by many countries is used to re-establish people in order to overcome their previous dependency. The range of programmes is many and various. Schemes that enable people to increase agricultural productivity are common. These may involve education, or practical help such as the installation of water pumps. In urban areas, there are housing improvements, skills training and general strategies to create self-supporting communities. In war zones one field of activity for aid agencies is the establishment of mine-clearing programmes, which enable people to return to their homes.

Source: Adapted from UNHCR, *Refugees*, April 1993

Aid generally falls into one of two categories. **Bilateral aid** is given directly by one government to another country. **Multilateral aid** comes from several or many governments and is often fed through a **donor agency** such as UNICEF (The United Nations Children's Fund) or the World Bank Group. Aid may be given in the form of either grants or loans. The latter, of course, has implications for future demands on the recipient because repayments must be made.

Some aid is for specific purposes and is known as **project aid**. Alternatively, it may be **programme aid**, given as general support for the full range of the government's activities. Loans may be **concessional**, which means that the rates of interest will be below those charged in the financial markets. **Non-concessional** loans are charged at the market rate.

Technical assistance is an alternative method of giving help to other countries. This involves sending people with specialist skills to assist with a particular development or to train the indigenous population.

The United Nations sets a target of 0.7% of GNP for developed countries to give as aid. Figure 2.1 shows that few achieve the UN's objective. Although the USA is the largest donor in terms of dollars, it comes almost bottom of the list when this figure is converted into a percentage of GNP.

Figure 2.1 Who are the donors?

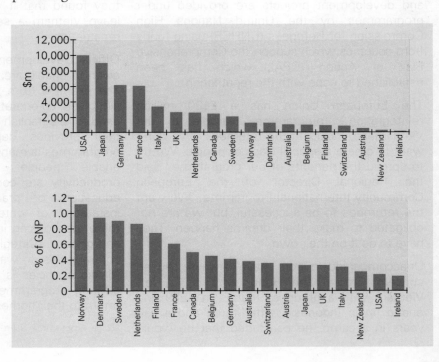

Source: *Human Development Report,* UN Development Program, 1992

2 Giving and receiving

Why give aid?

There are strong economic reasons for aid donations. Many of the recipient countries have a wealth of productive resources, but an inadequate supply of finance and foreign exchange with which to carry out investment projects. As a result, the resources are unproductive, when they could be helping to increase the growth rate for the country as a whole. This represents an imperfection in the capital market, because the supply of funds for investment does not reach those who can put it to use. There is a vicious circle: low investment leads to low incomes, from which little saving can be generated, so that there are few resources for investment. Aid can bridge the gap with the provision of both finance for capital expenditure and technical expertise.

Once the process is set in motion, incomes will increase and therefore gradually permit the population to increase saving. By doing this, the country slowly becomes able to fund further investment projects internally, instead of having to be supported by others. This is inevitably a long-term process, but the multiplier effect on the initial injection of assistance will generate further growth. Investment projects must be carefully chosen, so that those with the greatest potential returns are selected.

Technical expertise is often needed if new investment projects are to be carried out successfully. Many developing countries have a 'human resources gap', because education and training are not sufficiently sophisticated to enable people to cope with the technology employed. For aid to be effective, expertise must be passed to the local population so that the development becomes self-sustaining.

It is also suggested that the amount and nature of aid should be determined by a country's absorptive capacity. This relates to how effectively assistance will be used. There is, for example, little point in encouraging highly technical development when the long-term prospects for maintenance and support are poor.

Giving aid is not always an altruistic process. Donors often expect something in return. Both economic and political motives play a large part in the structure of international aid transfers. Assistance has been given to 'friendly' countries and those of strategic importance. Until the collapse of the Soviet Union, there was a clear divide between the flows of assistance to those countries which supported the East and those which supported the West.

Efficiency

Imperfect market

Human capital

Arms and the dam

A giant red crater has been scraped from the green Malaysian hillside. At the bottom, earth-moving machines crawl about like flies in a wound, sketching the outlines of the dam that will flood the verdant jungle behind. In two years, the water of the Pergau River and seven of its tributaries will drive turbines capable of generating 600 megawatts of electricity.

Demand for electricity arises from the country's inexorable economic growth. Even in Kelantan, one of Malaysia's poorest regions, the roads from the dam site to the capital are well-paved and filled with home-produced Proton cars.

This dam has swallowed £234 million of British taxpayers' money, equivalent to one-fifth of the British aid budget. The agreement was signed at the same time as a £1 billion arms deal was secured with Malaysia, by the prime minister in 1988.

It was pointed out that the orders won by Britain in Malaysia since 1988 have helped to preserve some 25,000 jobs. Although the Tornado deal was later cancelled, 28 Hawk trainers and ground-attack aircraft worth £400 million were ordered from British Aerospace.

Aid that is provided by governments is termed official development assistance, or ODA. Bilateral aid, which forms about 70% of all ODA, often has strings attached and is known as **tied aid**. This may be a formal part of the agreement or an implication of a particular type of support. A donor country may supply a developing country with funds or resources, but there may be a reciprocal agreement for the purchase of certain goods. The installation of a new factory will certainly help an emergent economy, but spare parts and updating will then have to be bought from the donor.

The recipients

Each year approximately $54 billion is given in aid, of which almost 98% comes from members of the OECD (Organisation for Economic Co-operation and Development). Figures 2.2 and 2.3 give a picture of the total aid received and how significant it is in terms of each country's economy.

Its allocation does not reflect need, as less than half the bilateral trade goes to the 46 countries with the lowest incomes. A comparison between Figures 2.2, 2.3 and 2.4 shows clearly that aid is not necessarily directed at the most needy. Egypt, which receives more aid than anywhere in the world, is thirty-seventh from the bottom of the league of low-income countries. It is given the equivalent of 17.2% of GNP, compared with a much poorer country such as Ethiopia, which receives 14.6% of its GNP from ODA. This pattern of development assistance suggests that politics and the economic interests of the donor countries are sometimes stronger considerations than the needs of the recipients.

Figure 2.2 The top 20 recipients: total aid

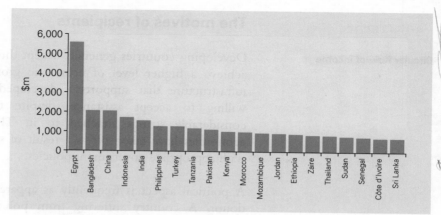

Source: World Bank, *World Development Report*, 1992

Figure 2.3 The top 20 recipients: aid as a percentage of their GNP

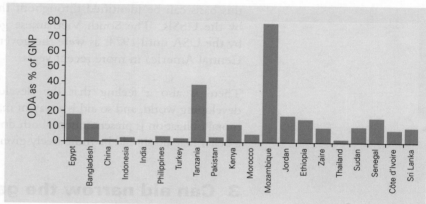

Source: World Bank, *World Development Report*, 1992

Figure 2.4 ODA to the poorest

Ten developing countries with highest number of poor	Number of poor (millions)	Poor as a % of world poor	ODA per capita ($)	ODA as a % of total ODA
India	410	34.2	1.8	3.5
China	120	9.9	1.8	4.7
Bangladesh	99	8.3	18.1	4.7
Indonesia	70	5.8	9.3	3.9
Pakistan	37	3.1	1.1	0.4
Brazil	33	2.8	1.1	0.4
Ethiopia	30	2.5	17.7	2.0
Myanmar	17	1.4	4.7	0.4
Thailand	17	1.4	14.1	1.8

Source: World Bank, *World Development Report*, 1992

The motives of recipients

Circular flow of income

Developing countries generally accept the view that aid is necessary to achieve a higher level of economic growth. Many are short of the infrastructure that supports a developed country and are therefore willing to accept assistance, despite the fact that it may have considerable strings attached to it. There are many cases where economies have taken off as a result of sustained injections combined with appropriate government policies.

A political aspect is frequently as apparent to the recipient as to the donor. A country suffering from political instability will generally welcome assistance that provides leverage to suppress opposition and so also enables it to remain in power. Countries that have accepted aid on this basis can be identified throughout the world. Cuba was supported by the USSR. The South Vietnamese government was kept in power by the USA until 1974, as were the governments of certain countries of Central America in more recent years.

There is also a feeling that the developed world has exploited the developing world, and so aid is a way of making recompense. This sense of moral obligation is present among both donors and recipients, and leads to a belief that aid should be more freely given and be less constrained.

3 Can aid narrow the gap?

Evaluating the effect of aid is not easy. The question that always crops up is 'What would have happened without it?'. The answer is not straightforward, for a variety of reasons. First of all, the type of aid that has been provided will affect the expected outcomes. Emergency aid is intended to provide short-term relief in crisis situations, and although it may contribute to re-establishing the economy, it is not a direct contributor to long-term growth. Figure 2.5 suggests that there is little relationship between the amount of aid as a proportion of GNP and the growth rate. In fact, the country that receives the highest percentage has negative growth, but this is Mozambique, which has been at war for many years. The country has been given support to help its population survive famine and injuries, rather than to encourage economic development.

The political conditions are therefore a second factor that complicates the picture. Among the top 20 aid recipients are several countries that are involved in conflict. The existing level of development will also have an effect on expectations. A country such as Burkina Faso in west Africa, which has virtually no natural resources, would be fortunate if aid helped

Open Question

What determines the
outcomes of giving aid?

it to make a small step forward. In a country that was provided with aid
to assist the exploitation of mineral resources, a more rapid pay-off would
be anticipated. The relationship between aid and growth is therefore
difficult to quantify with any precision. Suffice it to say that some
countries that have in the past received high levels of aid per capita, have
more recently achieved high growth rates. Thailand, South Korea and
Taiwan all fall into this category. There are, however, aspects of the whole
aid issue that raise questions about its effects and efficacy.

Figure 2.5 Aid and growth

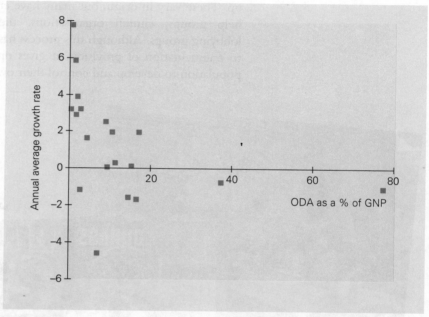

Source: World Bank, *World Development Report*, 1992

Does aid divide or unite?

Aid may divide society; some groups may benefit much more than
others, resulting in a dual society. The fear of the EU representative in
Vietnam was that by providing help for the returnees, others would be
disadvantaged and therefore create antagonism. As a result, a
programme was set up to assist a wider range of people.

Aid projects can cause rancour among the local population. Those who
are employed may receive a wage that is generous in local terms, but
below the level of the expatriate staff. This creates two possible sources
of discontent. Those with jobs in the new developments feel hard done
by, and those without feel even more unequal. In some cases the expert
staff who are brought in may live a very separate existence from the rest
of the community.

Does aid encourage an entrepreneurial culture?

It is argued that aid fails to develop the skills that lead to individuals functioning effectively in the complex markets of the developed world. Because the provision of assistance is often dealt with by government agencies, or by non-governmental organisations (NGOs) such as Oxfam, or by international bodies, there may be little opportunity for local people to learn to run their own projects. However, as the developed world has become less generous, many small domestic NGOs have sprung up. These vary in origin but many have emerged from trade unions, self-help groups, church organisations, the co-operative movement or lobbying groups. Although this process has drawbacks because it may lead to fragmentation of provision, it gives opportunities for the indigenous population to develop and control their own existence.

A travelling shop in Lima, Peru.

A watchmender's stand in Nigeria.

In some areas credit and marketing schemes have been set up. Success seems to come to the ones which promote labour-intensive trades and therefore open opportunities for small-scale industry to be established on a local basis. Such NGOs will also act as intermediaries and negotiators with the government, providers of aid and the area's élite.

Social and political change can help the supply of aid to be effective in promoting development. The generation of local earnings can assist the emergence of an entrepreneurial culture and a commercial framework. Small-scale developments are perhaps more likely to become an integral part of the local culture rather than forming a part of a dual economy.

Need or efficiency?

As the total amount of aid declines, the debate about its use becomes more pertinent. Should aid be given because there is a need for it, or should donations be evaluated on the basis of their effectiveness? Emergency aid is not generally questioned in this way because people need short-term relief in disaster situations.

Most projects have a considerable period devoted to planning and projection of outcomes and all donors insist that progress is monitored, but this is carried out within the remit of the donor organisation. Need and efficiency will be interpreted differently by different people and organisations. Countries with high levels of military expenditure receive about twice as much aid per capita as those with lower levels. The data have already shown that the poorest countries do not receive the bulk of the available aid. The drawback to the rather random allocation process is that assistance is unpredictable and is not related to human priorities.

Small-scale projects that help people to organise their own lives more effectively are often remarkably successful, as in the case of the revival of traditional work groups in Burkina Faso.

Groupement Naam

The Naam groups were set up in the Yatenga province of Burkina Faso, as a revival of traditional work groups. The basic idea is for the community to accumulate a production surplus and invest it in community development. During the rainy season, group activities include cultivating market garden plots and planting millet, cotton, sesame and groundnuts in communal fields. In the dry season, the focus shifts to soap making, textile production, animal husbandry and the production of fuel efficient ovens. After provision is made for depreciation and the capital needed for new investment, the profits are shared among group members.

The Naam groups also undertake various community works, digging ditches, rainwater storage tanks or small dams and tending community forests. The groups also promote sports and cultural activities and run literacy programmes. There are some 2,800 groups with more than 160,000 members. Their motto is 'development without damage'.

Source: *Human Development Report*, UN Development Program, 1993

Does aid reach its intended destination?

Who gets aid in the Third World?

Source: *South*, March 1984

Data on income distribution are not available for many very low income countries because there is often no system for its collection, so it is difficult to assess the effects of aid. There is strong evidence that a considerable proportion of aid provision goes astray and therefore never adds to the lives of those for whom it is intended. In Bangladesh, the World Food Programme aims to take food to the most impoverished groups, mainly through food for work schemes. Corruption would seem to be rife, as it appears that as little as 20% of the food reaches its intended objective. Much seems to be sold and the profits then line the pockets of local officials and contractors. The lack of accountability and the continuing source of supply enables corruption to persist. The aid supplies not only develop a dependency culture but also give those who process it opportunities to exercise power within their own systems. The gaps between rich and poor can grow as a result.

Debt: the outcome of aid?

Aid can be granted in the form of loans as well as grants. Borrowing necessitates repayments as well as incurring interest charges. Lending to developing countries by aid-giving organisations is generally on a **concessional** basis. In other words, the interest to be paid is lower than would be paid in the money markets. Tied aid, even as a gift, may cause difficulties because the recipient is committed, for example, to purchase machinery, from the donor country. The training of staff and maintenance will lead to further expense, which may have to be funded by borrowing. However, much of the debt that has exacerbated the problems of the developing world, has been the outcome of commercial borrowing, rather than being aid-associated.

4 Development or dependency?

Aid should lead a country towards a situation in which it can stand on its own feet. As this is achieved, the amount of financial assistance that is required should, therefore, diminish. There are, however, cases around the world that demonstrate that this is not happening. Bangladesh is second in the league of recipients, but the poor are getting poorer and the need for aid is increasing. About 80% of development projects and a substantial proportion of government spending are paid for from external sources. Aid is tempting to such countries, but if it is not directed effectively it will provide the wrong type of help. The parliament building, for example, was financed from external sources but has scarcely been used because of the political situation.

Investment

The parliament building in Dhaka.

Much aid money tends to be directed to prestige projects such as power-stations, bridges and major roads. These may have some indirect effect on the lives of most of the country's citizens. But many people would argue that what they really need is better healthcare, education and local infrastructure. Village roads have more significance to most of the population as they facilitate the movement of agricultural produce. With improved banking and credit, farming can become the source of growth to rural communities. The need is for small-scale projects, which allow people to use resources more effectively in order to have more control over their lives.

On the other hand, if a government wishes to attract investment from abroad, rather than aid, it will be necessary to develop the country's infrastructure. Modern industry is very dependent on good transport links. A UN report put it as follows: 'In most developing countries a lack of transport facilities is one of the main factors in world poverty and a major deterrent to rapid economic and social progress'. Without adequate transport, natural resources cannot be exploited, the growth of trade may be limited and therefore a country may be restricted in its ability to earn foreign currency, which is often a crucial part of the development process. Despite having only 30% of the world's population, the developed countries account for 88% of railway traffic and 72% of trucks and buses. The developing world would need 32 million kilometres of new roads, if it where to be on a par with the EU.

The provision of power supplies is essential to attract industry, but the building of power-stations does not necessarily affect most of the population. The more affluent residents of cities may benefit but the majority will find their lives unchanged. Without the infrastructure to carry electricity to rural areas, its use will be very constrained. Some countries that have low levels of consumption per capita, have become exporters of power. This attracts foreign currency, but does not help improve the standard of living for much of the population, and therefore reinforces the development of a dual economy.

The factors that facilitate the shift from dependency to development are complex and varied. The development of infrastructure alone is insufficient, but it appears to be one of the keys which triggers change. There is also debate about whether the development of large-scale infrastructure is the most effective way of moving to independence. The process of industrialising from the top down is criticised because it may lead to the creation of a dual economy. A view, which is strongly held by many, is that small-scale schemes that are within the scope and control of the local population will be more effective in the long term. The pace of change may be slower, but the outcomes will be more equitable and enduring.

Innovation

The case studies below concerning the jiko stove and small hydro-electric power units demonstrate one type of project in which aid is used to help the local community work more effectively. The technology being used in both cases is appropriate to the local environment, which has been studied carefully so that the projects can be self-sustaining. **Intermediate technology** is the term used to describe such developments, because the innovations employed are intermediate between traditional approaches and high technology. Intermediate technology often improves on existing techniques but does not use the highly sophisticated, capital-intensive methods found in the developed world. The stress is on use of existing skills and resources, so that people do not become over dependent on others.

The jiko: an energy efficient stove

The traditional Kenyan cooking stove, a jiko (Figure 2.6), had an energy efficiency of about 20%. As it ran on firewood, which was in increasingly short supply, a programme was set up to develop a more efficient model. A strategy was devised, which looked first at the requirements of the stove and its role in the life of users, in order to develop a product which was acceptable and effective. It was essential that the artisans who had made the traditional stove could continue the production process, so the second phase was a

Figure 2.6 Cross-section of a jiko

training programme for them and for people who demonstrate the new product in the community. The artisans were also provided with practical assistance to aid production. The final stage was monitoring and evaluation, so that constraints could be identified and impact assessed.

Social benefits

The total cost of the programme was about $500,000. Almost 100 new jobs were generated by the new processes, and households were estimated to be saving approximately $2 million. The demand for charcoal fell by 1.5 million tonnes per year and the toxic output was also reduced. This suggests that the stove provided a very high rate of return on the funds employed. The programme has been successful because of the involvement of local people in all stages of the process. It has enabled traditional cooking methods to continue, while using resources more effectively.

Power in Nepal

In rural areas of Nepal water power originally drove the grain mills. Recently diesel was introduced as a more flexible alternative. The drawback was the small output of power which can be generated by these small units. They were incapable of running more than one mill at a time, which was a problem because the four main crops require different types of machinery. As the demand for processed grains was rising, assistance was required. Small hydro-electric power plants were developed, in consultation with potential users, which could run three machines at a time. It was also possible to use these plants to establish small electrification schemes.

Once the development work was complete, credit was required if the machinery was to be used. Loans of 80% for up to ten years were switched from the diesel mills to the new water mills. Grants were made available to assist with electrification schemes.

Social costs and benefits

Cost savings, which have benefited both farmer and miller, have resulted from this innovation. To spread the savings more equitably, co-operatives are being established but as there is no legal framework for them in Nepal, progress is slow.

In the short term, the import of turbine equipment has a negative effect on the balance of payments, but this is outweighed by the reduction in the need for diesel. The environment also benefits because as electricity is installed, firewood is no longer required for cooking.

5 Can aid be more effective?

Although aid comes under heavy criticism from many sources, most recipient countries would take the view that they prefer more rather than less. To this end, the UN's aim for the developed world's contribution to the aid budget is 0.7% of total GNP. Few countries achieve anything like this amount, as was shown by Figure 2.1. A combination of 'aid-weariness' and recession in the developed world has created an environment in which countries have become more concerned about their domestic economies. It is difficult to persuade governments of the need for aid, when there is so much criticism of the process.

A flat rate of 0.7% would be inequitable because it means that the population of Ireland, with a per capita income of $8,710, would be providing the same percentage as Switzerland, where the figure is $29,880. To overcome this, the UN is looking for progressive proportions of GNP. Each country's target would be calculated by multiplying 0.7% by 1 plus the percentage difference between the donor's GNP per capita and the average GNP for all donors. Figure 2.7 shows the percentage of GNP each country would give under this system. The effect on the wealthiest countries is dramatic. In fact, if the United States and Japan met this request, 80% of the shortfall would have been made up. Figure 2.8 shows how much more or less, each country should be giving according to the UN.

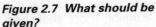

Figure 2.7 What should be given?

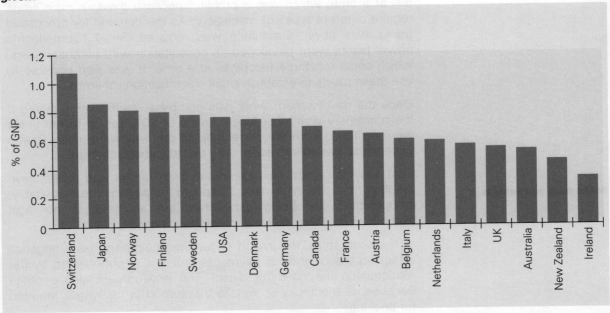

Source: *Human Development Report,* UN Development Program, 1992

Figure 2.8 How much more or less?

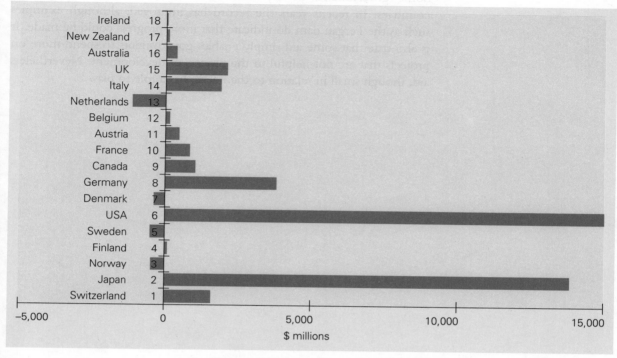

Source: *Human Development Report*, UN Development Program, 1992

Even if these figures are not achieved, the development of a more flexible system, in which aid was given with fewer constraints, would be beneficial. This would enable countries to decide which projects would stimulate the economy or help the population most effectively. It might remove the need for countries to take on enormous prestige projects, when smaller-scale developments using intermediate technology might be more appropriate.

An increasing proportion of ODA (official development assistance) is being passed through the large international assistance organisations. This is having a positive effect, because the money is less subject to the political leanings of individual countries and is more likely to come in the form of grants and concessional loans.

On balance...

Open Question

How should the idea of 'horses for courses' be applied when aid is allocated?

On a fundamental level, aid makes up for inadequate savings in low-income countries. It is in hard (i.e. convertible) currency, and can be used to purchase imported capital equipment. This widens the technological base of the economy. Growth depends on increasing the quantity and quality of resources; aid is useful because it can raise the quality of both labour and capital.

Some governments do try hard to direct aid towards the poorest countries. In recent years the record has improved, although examples such as the Pergau dam do indicate that more progress could be made. It is also true that some aid simply enables governments to spend more on projects that are not helpful to the process of development. Nevertheless aid, though small in relation to the needs, has a role to play.

Enquiry 3: Can trade reduce inequality?

Scope

The countries of the Pacific Rim have thrived on trade-based development. The question is, can this be the solution for everyone? This enquiry explores the effects that different trading strategies may have on the economies of the developing world. It seeks the positive and negative outcomes that occur in different countries, and their influence on both the individual and the economy as a whole.

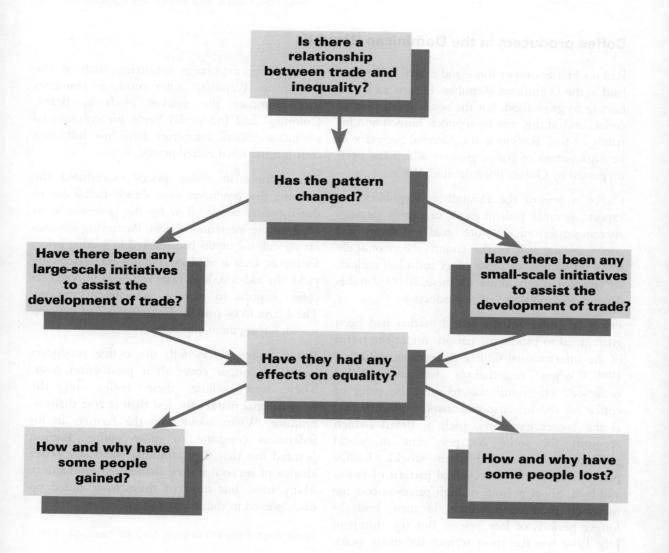

Opening evidence

US companies fire off a round of applause

Passage of the North America Free Trade Agreement by the House of Representatives was applauded by the US business community yesterday and roundly condemned by trade union officials.

Business leaders from many industry sectors praised the agreement, saying it would boost exports by US companies to Mexico and Canada, create jobs for American workers and enhance the role of the US.

In remarks that captured the general tone of the reaction, Mr John Smith, chief executive of General Motors, said: 'By saying Yes to Nafta, the House had made good on a great window of opportunity for America. For the first time, American-made products will be able to compete fairly in Mexico without the burden of tariffs and other barriers.'

Most union officials vowed to continue their fight against the agreement and repeated warnings to legislators who supported it. 'We need an agreement that affords workers the same protections which Nafta affords corporations.'

Source: Frank McGurty in the *Financial Times*, 19 November 1993

Coffee producers in the Dominican Republic

Rufino Herrera owns three and a half hectares of land in the Dominican Republic. He sets aside one hectare to grow food, but the rest is given over to coffee, and in this way he supports himself and his family of five. Rufino is also General Secretary of an organisation of coffee growers which has been supported by Oxfam since the mid-1980s.

Coffee is one of the Dominican Republic's key exports. It ranks fifth in terms of export earnings after sugar, ferronickel, dore (gold and silver), and cocoa. Nearly half of the country's economically active population, of a total of six and a half million, are engaged in agriculture. Of these, 70,000 families depend on small-scale coffee production.

Prices of coffee on the world market had been guaranteed to producing nations under the terms of the International Coffee Agreement until July 1989, when negotiations for its renewal collapsed. The result was to send the price of coffee on the international markets plummeting as the bigger exporters, such as Brazil (which accounts for some 30 per cent of world production), off-loaded their stocks. Coffee prices tend to follow a cyclical pattern of boom and bust. Short periods of high prices encourage increased production which, in turn, leads to longer periods of low prices. But the slump of July 1989 was the most serious for many years.

The smaller exporting countries, such as the Dominican Republic suffer most, as countries that dominate the market (such as Brazil, Colombia and Indonesia) battle for commercial advantage. Small countries have no influence over international coffee prices.

The collapse in coffee prices exacerbated the pressures that producers were already facing due to the measures being taken by the government to cope with its international debt. Removing subsidies on agricultural inputs had resulted in soaring prices for inputs, such as fertilisers and this led to declining yields. In addition, high taxes had been imposed on coffee exports to increase government revenue. These have to be paid by the farmer before the crop is sold, forcing them into debt.

When coffee prices fell, the coffee producers could no longer cover their production costs. They were selling their coffee on the international market for less than it cost them to produce. When asked why the farmers in his federation continue to grow coffee, Rufino pointed out that they wouldn't stand any better chance of survival if they abandoned production. Many have, but most of these have ended up unemployed in the shanty towns.

Source: Adapted from Belinda Coote, *The Trade Trap*, Oxfam, 1992

Shrimp production in Bangladesh

In recent years Bangladesh, one of the poorest and most densely populated countries in the world, developed a new export industry: shrimps. The industry is now well established, and is making a significant contribution to the country's foreign-exchange earnings. However, its development has entailed both social and environmental costs.

Unfortunately for Bangladesh, it was not the only country which diversified its economy into shrimp production during the 1980s. Shrimp production in Asia increased by more than 700 per cent between 1980 and 1988 – from a total of 57.2 thousand tonnes to 441.5 thousand tonnes. Bangladesh's industry, which increased production from 2.7 thousand to 25.0 thousand tonnes during that period, turns out to be only a very small fish in a very large sea. Other major Asian producers which have similarly boosted yields and exports during the 1980s are China, India, Indonesia, the Philippines, Taiwan, Thailand, and Vietnam, all of whom produce more than Bangladesh.

Source: Belinda Coote, *The Trade Trap*, Oxfam, 1992

Stars of the East

THE economic performance of these East Asian economies has been particularly dramatic, with their share of world exports of manufactures leaping from 9% in 1965 to 21% in 1990.

Not only did the eight economies grow rapidly, they were also successful in sharing the fruits of growth, with low and declining inequality of income. For example in South Korea the income of the richest 20% of households is eight times that of the poorest 20%. Compare that with Brazil or Mexico, where the richest fifth have at least twenty times as much income as the poorest fifth. In Malaysia the percentage of the population living in absolute poverty has dropped from 30% in 1960 to less than 5% in 1990; by contrast the percentage living in poverty in Brazil fell only from 50% to 21%.

Source: *The Economist*, 2 October 1993

Traidcraft: an alternative trading organisation

Richard Adams, founder of the British ATO, Traidcraft, describes his first big purchase from the Jute Works in Dhaka in 1974:

My first call the next morning was to the Jute Works. Information about my visit had failed to reach the people there, but they recognised me as one of their overseas customers, even though my order had been a small one. I explained that I hoped to buy enough handicrafts to fill up a large cargo plane. Disbelief turned to amazement and then to jubilant enthusiasm. The Jute Works took on the atmosphere of Santa's Workshop, with eager helpers rushing to fill up my sleigh! They would not have enough from their own stock: people would be sent to the village production centres and asked to send all they could. Would I take seconds? Would I take palm leaf mats, crochet work and embroidery? Would I take

bamboo furniture, cane baskets and sweeping brushes? Yes, I said, I would take almost anything that might sell in Britain, providing that it did not come to more than fifteen tonnes and one hundred cubic metres or £10,000 altogether.

The Jute Works is now entirely self-financing. Currently over 7,000 women are making goods for it. They are organised into small producer groups who buy their jute locally, or grow their own. The Jute Works gives them orders. It works with the women on design and quality control, as well as encouraging functional literacy classes. Its Group Development Fund encourages and assists with other forms of income generation including calf, goat and poultry rearing, sewing, rice cultivation, and fish farming. There is also a producers' provident security fund and a small credit project.

Source: Belinda Coote, *The Trade Trap*, Oxfam, 1992

1 To trade or not to trade?

Trade versus protectionism has been an issue ever since the human race began the process of exchange. It is the subject of debate in both developed and developing countries, as benefits and drawbacks can be identified for both individuals and nations. The question to be answered is: does trade reduce inequalities between rich and poor countries and between rich and poor people?

Absolute advantage

Often countries wish to protect a particular aspect of their economy or way of life. Free trade may be efficient in terms of allocating resources on a large scale, but the outcomes for sectors that are hit when someone else can produce goods more cheaply elsewhere can be devastating.

The French … their films and the GATT

FRANCE and other European countries have a language problem, which only occasionally has been surmounted by exile stars such as Maurice Chevalier, Dietrich and Garbo. It is hard, indeed almost impossible for a French film to achieve the international acclaim of say Howard's End or The Remains of the Day.

The French pitched their argument at the GATT negotiations carefully: while professing their love for Hollywood, they also fought to hang on to their own national creativity, even if it cannot, by itself, be profit-making.

Film-making in France costs about 3 billion francs (£350 million) a year. The industry's receipts are about 4 billion francs, 11% of which comes from a tax on cinema tickets, 5.5% from television licences and advertising, and 2% from a tax on the sales of video cassettes.

The Americans argued that the proceeds from the French taxes should be shared. It was a David and Goliath struggle but the French won the day.

Source: Adapted from the *Daily Telegraph*, 15 December 1993

… and their music

The music industry in France is to be subject to a law which tells it that radio stations must broadcast a minimum of 40% French music a month. At least half this quota must be composed of rising new talent. M. Javier Pons, the secretary-general of the Association for French Radio Stations is violently opposed to the new ruling and is taking advice as to its legality in a European context.

The two examples from France show how a country that is deprived of the economies of scale, generated by world markets, can find it difficult to compete. Sales of French films and music are small beyond the French-speaking world, but are regarded as an important part of the country's cultural development. In an attempt to protect this aspect of

Trade barriers

The infant industry argument for protection

Comparative advantage

Economies of scale

French life, the government fought the GATT agreement, which would have denied them the right to tax imported films and use the money to subsidise their own industry.

In a broader context, the objective of protection is the same. Industries may, for a variety of reasons, be unable to compete in world markets. For political and economic purposes governments can set up systems of tariffs or quotas, which create a wall that prevents or discourages the import of cheaper versions of the product. Some countries have used this technique to allow new industries to become established.

The Japanese achieved high levels of economic growth in industries that were developed from scratch after the Second World War. By preventing the entry of equivalent products from the developed world, they enabled growth to take place on a strong home base.

To achieve this growth, the Japanese had to make decisions about their future direction. They opted, against the advice of the USA, to develop high-tech industries rather than the primary products in which they then had a comparative advantage. Their objective was to promote industries that would produce goods for export. Through this policy, they have achieved their current status as one of the richest countries in the world.

The combination of protecting the home market while selling energetically into other markets might be more difficult to achieve today, as the world has developed a sophisticated regime of trade agreements.

Countries can generally be classified by their attitude towards trade as a focus for development. The outward looking **export-promoters** encourage a free movement of goods and money, whereas the **import-substitutors** seek the development of domestic industries by the use of import controls. Figure 3.1 on page 48 shows how they stood in the 1980s. Some have now shifted towards a more outward-oriented approach.

The strongly outward-oriented countries look to the world economy as the market for the sale of both their primary products and their manufactured goods. The moderately outward-looking countries have the same aim, to a lesser degree. The cost structures of their industries benefit from the economies of scale that can be gained by selling into such large markets. The term 'free-traders' is not totally appropriate, as even the most committed exporters have resorted to protectionist policies in certain industries at certain times.

Import-substitutors plan, initially, to replace imports of simple consumer goods with their home-produced equivalents. Over time, the

Strongly outward-oriented	Moderately outward-oriented	Moderately inward-oriented	Strongly inward-oriented
Hong Kong	Brazil	Cameroon	Argentina
Rep. of Korea	Chile	Colombia	Bangladesh
Singapore	Israel	Costa Rica	Bolivia
	Malaysia	El Salvador	Burundi
	Thailand	Guatemala	Dominican Rep.
	Tunisia	Honduras	Ethiopia
	Turkey	Indonesia	Ghana
	Uruguay	Ivory Coast	India
		Kenya	Madagascar
		Mexico	Nigeria
		Nicaragua	Peru
		Pakistan	Sri Lanka
		Philippines	Sudan
		Senegal	Tanzania
			Yugoslavia
			Zambia

Source: World Bank, *World Development Report*, 1987

Figure 3.1 Export-promoters or import-substitutors?

country would progress to more complex goods, with the eventual hope of becoming an exporter. To carry out these plans, tariff walls would be necessary in order to protect these infant industries. The aim is to achieve balanced growth by encouraging a diversified range of industries to become established. This avoids the trap of over concentration in one sector, which has held back some developing countries. The moderately inward-looking countries are seeking a degree of self sufficiency.

2 Export promotion: a source of growth?

Developing manufacturing industry

The countries in Figure 3.2 show varying rates of growth in relation to a rapid rate of growth of trade. Many demonstrate a strong correlation between increasing trade and economic growth. Even those that have slowed down since 1980 are still growing relatively quickly when compared with highly developed countries.

Production possibility frontier

Countries such as South Korea, Hong Kong and Singapore have all grown at astounding rates on the basis of manufactured exports. In South Korea, for example, manufactures contributed 80% of the country's foreign-exchange earnings.

Figure 3.2 Growth and trade

Country	Average annual growth rate GDP		Export growth	Import growth
	1970–80	1980–91	1980–91	1980–91
Bangladesh	2.3	4.3	7.2	4.3
China	5.2	9.4	11.5	9.5
Pakistan	4.9	6.1	9.9	2.6
Paraguay	8.5	2.7	12.2	5.8
Thailand	7.1	7.9	14.1	11.1
Malaysia	7.9	5.7	10.9	7.2
Portugal	4.3	2.9	11.1	10.0
Korea	9.6	9.6	12.2	11.1

Source: World Bank, *World Development Report*, 1992

Machinist in a textile factory, Singapore.

It must be remembered, however, that this was not achieved on the basis of a free market. These countries have had strong development plans that have involved some high tariffs to protect their burgeoning industries, just as Japan did before them. They have also faced difficulties in selling as effectively as they might wish in the markets of the developed world, because of the tariff barriers they face there. Their success demonstrates how effectively they have succeeded in undercutting the prices of similar products produced by these higher-cost economies.

The products for which import controls have been most severe are those that provide the greatest threat to the labour force of the developed world. Industries that use high levels of relatively unskilled labour, such as the footwear and textile industries, have been protected by tariffs. It is these very products in which the developing world has a comparative advantage, and which would allow entry level competition in a world market for less sophisticated developing countries.

Tunisia: looking outwards

Tunisia's export record in the 1980s has been impressive, not so much in volume but in composition. The balance has shifted from raw materials to manufactured goods – a change of direction which profited greatly from early investment in human development.

Until the 1980s, the bulk of export income came from oil and phosphates. But with the collapse of world prices and declining reserves, exports had dropped 30% by 1986. A dynamic manufacturing sector, which emerged in the 1970s, expanded to fill the gap so that total exports are now back at the 1980 level.

The average rate of manufacturing growth between 1965 and 1989 was 8.4% a year, and manufacturing value added has been one of the highest in Africa – 16% of GDP. This growth was accompanied by rises in productivity of 2% a year in the 1980s – so wages could rise as well.

This dynamism was possible only because

Tunisia had made human development a priority. A healthy and educated population provides an efficient workforce. Tunisia has made more progress in this respect than many other (generally wealthier) Arab states. Life expectancy is greater than average and under five mortality per 1,000 live births fell between 1960 and 1990 from 254 to 62.

Tunisia has made similar advances in education. Adult literacy is now 65%. Tunisia's women have made significant progress. The women's literacy rate in the average Arab state is only 63% of the male rate, while in Tunisia the figure is 76% – and rising.

Tunisia still has growing problems of unemployment and underemployment but its higher levels of human development leave it well positioned to benefit from trade opportunities in the 1990s.

Source: *Human Development Report*, UN Development Program, 1992

Few countries have been as successful as Tunisia in making the shift from being a commodity producer to a manufacturer. As the *Human Development Report* suggests, there have been other factors that have contributed to this growth. Tunisia has achieved more than many other developing countries in adapting to world markets, but is unlikely to achieve the status of a 'newly industrialised economy' (NIE).

These fast growing economies, which have all succeeded in diversifying exports, may, however, not provide a model for others to emulate. They were never among the poorest countries, and it is generally accepted that richer countries grow faster than poorer ones. There is also no assumed relationship between rapid, trade-related growth and improvements in living standards for the population in general. In fact, the drive for industrial expansion may lead to increased hardship for some sectors of the population, at least in the short to medium term. The other area that has to be taken into account is the impact that such growth may have on the environment. In Thailand, for example, Bangkok has become a hectic urban centre, containing all the features to be found in a city of the developed world. But industrialisation, which has resulted from the country's desire to compete in world markets, has created very different outcomes for other members of the population. Inequality has increased as the rural population has suffered from loss and degradation of the land. The outcomes have been poverty, malnutrition and a flight to the cities. Had trade not been the driving force behind the process of industrialisation, the damage might have been less severe.

Source: Mark Bryant (ed.), *Turn Over a New Leaf*, Earthscan, 1990

Export-led growth usually improves the standard of living of those involved in industry. The trickle-down effect seems slow to operate and the rural poor appear to gain less. The time period involved, however, is as yet, short. Many of these countries have only recently moved into a period of rapid growth, and the effects may take longer to work through to the population as a whole. In Hong Kong, which is a relatively small community, a degree of improvement in the standard of living of the majority of the population has become apparent.

The rapid growth that has been associated with export promotion in Pacific Rim countries can cause externalities within the country. Rural communities in Thailand, which has recently joined the Asian tigers, have borne the brunt of this rapid expansion. Although growth in general may cause such side effects, the speed with which export-led growth takes place magnifies the problem.

Thailand: internal effects of looking out

The Karen people form the largest tribal minority group in Thailand. They are shifting cultivators, who inhabit the hills along the country's border with Mayanmar (formerly Burma). There are no areas that are reserved for tribal minorities, so the land that the Karen used to regard as their territory has steadily been overtaken by farming, forestry and industry. Because the land is not legally theirs, Thai farmers have been able to move in and take over with no challenge.

The development of forestry reserves by the government has reduced the area in which the Karen can continue their shifting cultivation. Government policy has been to stop the tribes moving about and protect the forests. All that they have succeeded in doing is to reduce the area in which they can shift.

The third challenge to their existence has been industrial development. Roads have been built, which permit access to areas that have now been exploited for minerals and logging. Apart from impinging on the tribal lands, these developments have affected the watersheds and have resulted in pollution and soil erosion.

Many of the Karen have been reduced to poverty and malnutrition. Some of the young men have left to work in the mines and tea plantations. There has been a steady flow of young women to the cities, where many have joined Thailand's growing population of prostitutes.

The environmental impact

The movement of the farmers to the land that was formerly inhabited by the Karen has created a growing problem of soil erosion. The soil in the hills is poor and the farmers do little to aid its conservation. Farmers should be rotating their crops so that the soil's fertility can be rebuilt, but few do so. This is leading to a breakdown in the soil structure and a steady fall in productivity, particularly in rice production. Weed control is scarcely practised and therefore exacerbates the situation. As more land is cleared, the problems deepen. Attempts have been made to increase the rice yield using fertiliser, but to little effect.

There have been serious effects off-site as well. Forestry has suffered from the spread of farmland both into areas that were previously wooded and those that have been left to lie fallow. Soil erosion has led to the siltation of water courses and reservoirs, reducing water storage capacity and output of hydroelectric power. The drainage system has been degraded and floods have resulted in places as far away as Bangkok. As rivers become shallower, shipping is restricted and dredging has to be carried out.

Figure 3.3 The highland forests of Thailand

Can exporting primary products lead to growth?

The objective of development based on primary products is fraught with difficulty. As prices have fallen on world markets and the terms of trade continue to move against such producers, countries have been left in a dilemma over whether to increase output, which of course, may make the price fall further, or to diversify.

Producers face the problem that both price and income elasticities of demand for foodstuffs are low. As the world grows richer, the proportion of income that people spend on food declines, and as the population of the developed world is relatively stable, an increase in demand is not going to be achieved from this source. A fall in price simply frees up more money to spend on other things. Producers probably find that revenue falls when the price falls.

The development of synthetic substitutes has eroded the market for many of the world's natural products. This has, of course, added to the fall in the market price and has compounded the problems of producers.

Attempts to organise producers to collaborate in controlling supply, in their own group interests, have had little success. The commodity

Price elasticity of demand and supply

Income elasticity of demand

agreements that have been established have generally failed to achieve the objectives of regulating the market and maintaining stability in both price and levels of production.

Customs unions

The development of trading blocs such as the EU discriminates against the developing world, because assistance is given to farmers within the Union and tariffs are set against imports. Divisions are also created outside the EU, because some countries have preferential access, due to historic colonial links with member countries.

The degree of dependence on commodities as a source of income leaves much of the world in a very vulnerable position. The map of Africa in Figure 3.4 shows the percentage of commodities in each country's export earnings.

Figure 3.4 Commodity dependence in Africa

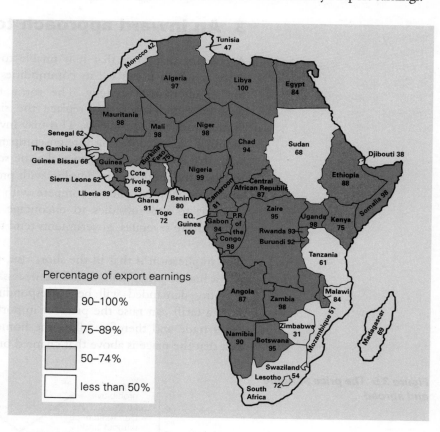

Percentage of export earnings

- 90–100%
- 75–89%
- 50–74%
- less than 50%

Source: World Bank, *Global Economic Prospects*, 1991

A further problem of fragmented land tenure (i.e. very small farms) makes the production process inefficient and slows the adoption of modern techniques, which are generally more appropriate to large-scale farms and plantations. If, on the other hand, production is plantation-based, little benefit may accrue to the local labour force, particularly when world prices are falling; there will be a constant pressure to reduce costs and employment.

These problems make it very difficult for a country to take the step to effective development on the basis of primary production alone. What is needed is usually a co-ordinated approach that encourages both agricultural and industrial development. Some countries have no choice but to depend on their primary export earnings in the early days of development. However, the development process itself changes the pattern of comparative advantage. Previously impossible strategies become possible. Some developing countries are producing vegetables, which sell for high prices in developed countries' markets. These are still primary products, but they are more profitable than the traditional commodity exports. The development of this trade requires good transport links. Aid-financed roads and airports can open up unexpected markets. Later on in the development process the comparative advantage in manufactures may develop, as happened in the Asian tigers.

3 An inward approach to success?

A country that finds that it is unable to develop because of the low price at which it can sell its commodities in world markets, must look for an alternative strategy. The route that many have taken is to encourage industries that replace the simpler imported goods with home-produced equivalents. This may involve developing home-grown industries or encouraging foreign companies to set up within the tariff walls that must be erected to make the scheme work. The objective is to allow the industries to develop with protection in the hope that they will eventually be able to compete with outsiders. It is, in fact, more efficient to use subsidies to encourage such industries, but because tariffs create revenues, governments tend to prefer them.

The implication is that in the short run, the home market will have to pay a higher price than would be necessary if trade were free, and the quantity demanded will be correspondingly small. Figure 3.5 shows how a tariff can raise the price of imported goods to a point that will deter trade and therefore allow the home market to grow, despite the fact that the price is above that charged on the world market.

Figure 3.5 The price at home and abroad

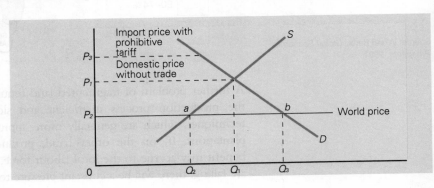

Computer start-up

The Brazilian computer industry had been dependent on foreign firms, which either imported finished products or had set up 'screwdriver' factories, completing assembly in the country.

Few people believed that a successful industry could be developed from scratch, but the Brazilian government decided to make an attempt. In order to create a protected environment for the new industry it set up a 'reserved market' in which only Brazilian-owned firms could participate. This meant that firms had to be 100% Brazilian in order to produce small and medium-sized computers and their peripherals.

The protection that was provided for this 'infant industry' led to a range of beneficial developments:

- The skills base in technological industries grew rapidly as firms were involved in extensive research and development.
- Companies with specific connections, such as to the banking system, became innovative and developed specialist skills.
- The national firms had much more influence in the international market place than any firm had previously. International companies were prepared to transfer technology on better terms.

- As the industry grew, externalities developed with the increased number of companies providing inputs.

There were losses as well as gains:

- Brazilians were forced to use less sophisticated equipment than was available elsewhere.
- Prices were higher than outside the reserved market (see Figure 3.5) but were constantly falling as the technology developed.
- The industry was product-led rather than consumer-led.

Despite the disadvantages and the constant crises of the Brazilian economy, the development was successful beyond expectations. In 1977 there were four firms operating in the nationally owned computer industry. By 1986, this figure had risen to 310 firms, which had a 51% share of the total computer market. Employment had risen from 4,000 to 40,000 and created a pool of technically skilled people.

Recently all protection was removed and imports became free to enter the country. Prices fell. Some firms have survived, some have gone to the wall and others have become involved in joint ventures. In the long run, the industry's survival is an open question.

The success of the Brazilian computer firms has not been repeated generally. Their determination to develop a national industry led large companies to treat them differently. Most developing countries that attempt to break into this market face determined opposition. The protection of intellectual property rights has strengthened in recent years, thus preventing access into the highly sophisticated technologies of the developed world. All the major computer companies spend millions of pounds every year on research and development, amounts that are inconceivable for many developing countries. Their markets are not large enough to sustain such investment, and the costs of buying into the latest technology and adapting it to their needs is often prohibitive. The only route available is usually to encourage the foreign companies to invest in their country.

In many countries, attempts to establish industries under protection have been largely regarded as a failure. This is particularly true of Latin America.

There are a number of causes of this failure, which range from the motives of trans-national corporations to the comfortable lives that protected industries have behind the tariff wall. These are shown in Figure 3.6.

Figure 3.6 Why does import substitution often fail?

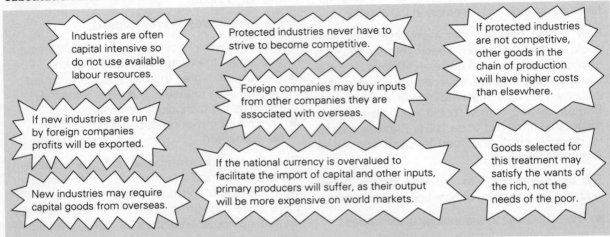

Industries are often capital intensive so do not use available labour resources.

Protected industries never have to strive to become competitive.

If protected industries are not competitive, other goods in the chain of production will have higher costs than elsewhere.

Foreign companies may buy inputs from other companies they are associated with overseas.

If new industries are run by foreign companies profits will be exported.

If the national currency is overvalued to facilitate the import of capital and other inputs, primary producers will suffer, as their output will be more expensive on world markets.

Goods selected for this treatment may satisfy the wants of the rich, not the needs of the poor.

New industries may require capital goods from overseas.

4 The impact of trading blocs and agreements

GATT

This excerpt from *The Economist*, published during the week of the final agreement on GATT's Uruguay Round explains why the lengthy negotiations were worth the trouble and also gives dissenting views. The GATT agreements are based firmly on the theory of comparative advantage. The objective is to free international trade, thus reducing imperfections in the market which deprive people of the opportunity to purchase goods at the lowest efficient prices.

AFTER years of exhausting negotiation, GATT has come right. Does it matter? A certain weariness is apparent. Some advocates of free trade feel that the agreement is, in the end, a let down – that it falls far short of what it might have achieved, that the compromises needed to bring the talks to a conclusion render it worthless. From another side it is argued that the deal will spur trade and industrial country growth and is therefore a downright bad thing: more trade pollutes the planet, while making the rich richer and the poor poorer (it is hard to say what causes greater offence). A third school of thought agrees that the deal will spur trade and that this is a bad thing, not because it will hurt the poor, but because it will help them and thus hurt the rich. Assailed on all sides by such arguments, the uncommitted may be forgiven for asking whether the agreement was worth the trouble.

Source: *The Economist*, 18 December 1993

The Uruguay Round, with 117 participants and an agreement that stretches to 500 pages, has contributed to freedom of trade in a number of ways. It:

■ succeeded in cutting tariffs by around 40%, which is significantly better than the one-third reduction that was sought;
■ made agricultural tariffs more explicit. The EU's Common Agricultural Policy has always been a bone of contention, because it gives European farmers high levels of subsidy and protection;
■ brought intellectual property rights within the system;
■ opened up some government purchases to international competition;
■ relaxed the rules on cross-border investment;
■ streamlined the world's trading system.

It is estimated that all these movements towards trade liberalisation should add $213 billion (at 1992 prices) to world income in the year 2002 and each year after that date. These benefits will, however, be unequally distributed, as shown in Figure 3.7. OECD countries, for example, will gain almost two-thirds of the total.

Figure 3.7 Winners and losers from the GATT trade round

	% change in real income 2002	
	Effect of GATT round	Full free trade
Low-income Asia	0.6	1.3
China	2.5	1.5
India	0.5	1.8
Upper-income Asia	2.6	8.2
Indonesia	−0.7	−2.6
Other Africa	−0.2	−0.9
Nigeria	−0.4	−1.8
South Africa	0.6	0.1
Maghreb	−0.5	−2.3
Mediterranean	−0.4	−2.4
Gulf region	0.5	−1.0
Other Latin America	0.6	1.3
Brazil	0.4	0.4
Mexico	0.0	−0.4
United States	0.2	0.3
Canada	0.2	0.0
Australia/New Zealand	0.1	1.0
Japan	0.9	2.7
European Union	1.4	2.8
Eastern Europe	0.1	−0.1
Former Soviet Union	0.1	0.9

Source: OECD and World Bank

The losers appear to be some of the poorest parts of the world. It has been estimated that $7 billion a year might be lost to sub-Saharan Africa, North Africa and the Mediterranean countries. This may not sound a great deal compared to the gains, but the average per capita income in black Africa is only $280 per year.

Some of these effects come from the reduction in farm subsidies in Europe, which will lead to higher prices on world markets. Production in low-cost areas will rise as a result, but will lead to losses for countries that import more than they export. The data for complete free trade shows how the removal of subsidies would accentuate the process already discussed.

Open Question

Have the effects of the Uruguay Round become apparent yet?

Although both the OECD and the World Bank estimate that Europe will gain from the agreement, others suggest that it will speed the movement of industrial production to low labour-cost economies. This would, of course, have a negative effect on the mature economies of Europe. In the same week that the GATT deal was agreed, General Motors confirmed a major investment in Poland, which probably shows the pattern for the future. The outcome of this may well be greater inequality between individuals within the developed economies in Europe, but a greater degree of equality between nations.

The European Union

The European Union is a customs union, which has steadily removed trade barriers between the member countries while maintaining an external tariff against imports from the rest of the world. This not only discriminates against other developed countries, but also has a negative effect on trade with the developing world. It is estimated that the European Union, together with other trade agreements in the developed world, reduces other countries' GNP by 3%, or a total of $75 billion. The structure of the EU's external tariffs is designed to discourage primary producers from processing their products. Raw coffee, tea or sugar, for example, will be subject to a much lower tariff than if it is ready for the shelves of the supermarket. This protects the European food-processing industry and prevents the producing countries from earning the greater rewards that result from adding value to the raw materials.

Members of the EU had strong trade links with their colonies, often to the extent that the latter had become dependent. In theory these should have been severed when the Treaty of Rome, which established the European Community, was signed by the original six members. In order to overcome the political problems that would result, the Treaty gave these colonies continued rights to trade and aid. As the countries became independent, a series of Conventions, concluding with the Lomé Convention, continued this special relationship. The 69 members are from Africa, the Caribbean and the Pacific (ACP). Many of them have continued to be highly dependent on trade with the EU, and any suggestion that the relationship should end causes uncertainty about the future of their economies.

Diversification is not always straightforward. Tourism seems an obvious alternative for islands in sunny climes, but it can be very disruptive to the social structure and may generate political instability.

Caribbean slips on a banana skin

CARIBBEAN banana growers will hear this month whether they have won one of the world's greatest trade wars.

At stake is an 18-year-old protective agreement, which allows Windward Island Fruit to enter the UK duty free, while limiting the number of bananas imported from Latin America.

If, as growers on St Lucia, Grenada, St Vincent and Dominica fear, the decision in Geneva goes against them and the market is flooded with cheap fruit, many may have to abandon their traditional way of life and cash in on the island's growing tourist trade.

The threat to remove EU protection, plus competition from bigger more efficiently produced South American bananas, have caused prices to slump. In St Lucia, tourists were warned to keep off the main roads after local farmers rioted in protest at falling wages.

In Grenada, banana prices have fluctuated, prompting many locals to leave the fields and work instead in hotels, bars and shops.

In September last year, Geest plc, which imports bananas from the Windward Islands, reported a collapse in profits for the previous six months. A spokesman said 'Growers have got used to a certain level of income and they are concerned that falling prices will lead to a drop in their living standards.'

There are also fears that if tourism fails to fill the gap left by banana production,

some islanders may turn to the sale and smuggling of drugs.

Dominica, which depends on bananas for 70% of its foreign-exchange earnings, has said that without the money generated by the sale of fruit, the economy will become unstable.

While tourism may provide jobs, the danger is that fast development may destroy the atmosphere of traditional Caribbean life that visitors find so attractive. The root of the problem is in British policy of the 1930s and 1940s, when colonies were encouraged to move into banana cultivation in an attempt to prevent social unrest.

In the 1980s farmers were encouraged to plant new fields, despite the uncertain future of the industry. Under the traditional system, the British ate bananas from the English-speaking Caribbean islands and the French bought those from their dependencies of Guadeloupe and Martinique, and the deficit in demand was made up by the 'dollar' bananas from South and Central America.

Latin American producers want an extra 200,000 tonnes over two years, to be allowed into Europe at a low tariff, in

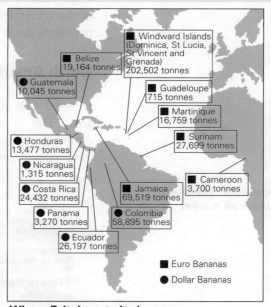

Where Britain gets its bananas

Belize 19,164 tonnes

Windward Islands (Dominica, St Lucia, St Vincent and Grenada) 202,502 tonnes

Guatemala 10,045 tonnes

Guadeloupe 715 tonnes

Martinique 16,759 tonnes

Honduras 13,477 tonnes

Surinam 27,699 tonnes

Nicaragua 1,315 tonnes

Costa Rica 24,432 tonnes

Cameroon 3,700 tonnes

Jamaica 69,519 tonnes

Panama 3,270 tonnes

Colombia 58,895 tonnes

Ecuador 26,197 tonnes

■ Euro Bananas
● Dollar Bananas

addition to the present quota of 2 million tonnes. The head of the Union of Banana Exporting Countries has claimed that EU restrictions have already cost $100,000 in Latin America.

To try to fill the gap left by the fall in revenue from bananas, all of the Windward Islands have been making strenuous attempts to encourage foreign tourists. Grenada has increased visitors by 10% this year to 66,400. The chairman of the tourist board said 'It is our job to encourage development. Last year there were 1,700 school-leavers looking for jobs. Next year there will be 2,200.'

· Source: Adapted from *The Times*, 6 January 1994

Competition

Structural change

The Lomé Convention has created a no–win situation. It was established to help countries that had colonial links with the EU and whose economies had come to depend on this trading relationship. It has resulted in a continued over–dependence and a resulting failure to diversify. Countries outside have become more efficient because they have had to compete in a tougher market, and they deeply resent their inability to sell their output on equal terms in Europe.

Bringing the system to an abrupt end would be disastrous for these dependent economies, so the concessions are reviewed at regular intervals. This will allow time for structural adjustments, such as the development of tourism, to take place. A positive feature of the Lomé Convention is Stabex, which is a fund designed to stabilise the earnings of the 69 ACP countries. It uses the European Development Fund and payments made by countries when their export earnings are high.

North American Free Trade Agreement

In 1993 Canada, the USA and Mexico agreed to create a free-trade area. This is expected to improve growth prospects for all three countries, bringing substantial structural change in the process. Figure 3.8 shows the existing trading relationships between the three.

Figure 3.8 The North American market

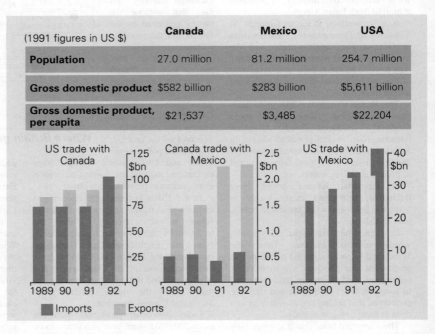

(1991 figures in US $)	Canada	Mexico	USA
Population	27.0 million	81.2 million	254.7 million
Gross domestic product	$582 billion	$283 billion	$5,611 billion
Gross domestic product, per capita	$21,537	$3,485	$22,204

Sources: OECD; IMF

The fear that investment and therefore jobs would move to the low-wage economy of Mexico caused the fight to be hard, and the margin of votes for the measure in the US House of Representatives was small.

The agreement removes tariffs between Mexico, Canada and the USA. While the economic structure of the first two is similar, Mexico is a more affluent developing country. Figure 3.9 shows the disparity in wages.

Figure 3.9 Hourly wage rates for production workers in manufacturing in the USA and Mexico

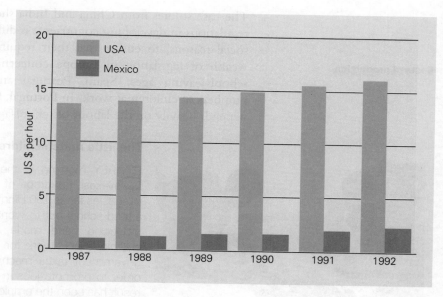

Source: US Department of Labor

From some points of view, the anxieties of the Americans were hard to understand. The Mexican economy is equivalent to only 4% of that of the United States, its level of productivity is far lower and its workforce is poorly educated and ill-equipped. There will no doubt be some job losses in the USA because low-skilled jobs will move to Mexico but equally, as the Mexican economy benefits from free trade it will grow and generate more demand for its neighbour's products. If the textile industry suffers, the motor industry and others producing consumer goods will gain. This demonstrates clearly how a change for the greater good can result in individual suffering.

Comparative advantage

The lobbyists have helped to create an agreement, which, in the words of the US Trade Representative, is 'new, unique and stunning in terms of trade agreements.' It has, built into it, a process for reviewing business compliance with each nation's environmental laws as well as wage regulations and trade conditions. Environmental organisations will be able to appeal against companies that are perceived to be moving to Mexico because of their weaker regulations.

5 Can the playing-field ever be level?

The NAFTA agreement has raised issues that have never been addressed before on an official level. One of the fears of the developed world as trade becomes freer, is that their industry will lose out because it is subject to many more stringent controls than those of the developing world. There are regulations that deal with wages, health and safety, the use of motor vehicles, and the effect on the environment – to name but a few.

Private and external costs

The case studies from China and India show that even when there are regulations in developing countries it is difficult, for both economic and social reasons, to ensure that their requirements are met. Despite the wealth of legislation in Europe concerning conditions of work and school-leaving ages, Spain, Portugal and Italy all have significant numbers of children at work. In Portugal, for example the shoe industry depends heavily on the labour of school-age children.

Costs of production

Young children fill frames of matches.

The little match children

EARLY morning in the dusty south Indian town of Sivakasi, hundreds of buses disgorge children from villages as far as 100 kilometres away. They come not to attend school but to work in thousands of tiny factories producing hand made matches. They handle toxic chemicals and work for up to 60 hours a week. The government taxes machine made matches heavily, in order to promote jobs in the hand made industry. One result has been the employment of 80,000 children. Past attempts to ban child labour in various industries have not worked. Poor families need the income of children, whatever the law says. The latest study shows that half the Sivasaki match industry families would fall below the poverty line if children were stopped from working.

Source: *The Economist*, 15 January 1994

Chinese workers die in factory fire

A fire that swept through a doll factory in the Chinese boom town of Shenzhen killed 81 workers and injured 36. The workers, mainly impoverished women migrants, could not escape because the doors and windows were locked. This had been done to keep the workers inside.

The official *Shenzhen Special Zone Daily* reported that the municipal fire department had sent a notice asking for improvements to be implemented six months ago but they had never been carried out.

Factory fires, due to poor safety standards, have killed more than 170 people in the area in the last two years. This blaze was the third major fire in Shenzhen in four months. One government official accused foreign investors of trying to 'save money by installing below standard safety facilities' and said that the partner of the Hong Kong investors was helping authorities with their investigations.

Source: *The Sunday Times*, 21 November 1993

Poor working conditions in developing countries create two fears in developed countries. First, the ability of developing countries to export goods more cheaply because of weaker controls makes competition more difficult. Secondly, these countries could become popular locations for investment. Regulation means that external costs are turned into private costs, and therefore production in the developed world is more expensive. It would be tempting for companies to establish factories in places where the rules are minimal. This was the main objection of American trade unionists, when faced with NAFTA.

The theory of comparative advantage fails to take such differentials into account, as no distinction is made between prices that cover social costs and those that do not. If Portugal can make shoes more cheaply than Germany because it is using cheap child labour, trade takes place.

The World Bank, in its *World Development Report* gives general policy advice that if markets are working smoothly, they should be allowed to continue, but if imperfections appear, corrective action should be taken:

- Competition should be protected through anti-monopoly legislation, which should be policed efficiently because it is never villain-proof.
- Consumers should be protected by legislation to control product safety; e.g. in the pharmaceutical, food and motor industries.
- Workers should be protected by trade unions and legislation.
- Specific groups, such as women and ethnic minorities, should be protected and enabled to take their rightful role in the market.
- The environment should be protected to prevent its degradation.

6 Does trade lead to equality?

Trade and income distribution

This enquiry has demonstrated ways in which trade leads to both equality and inequality. Trade theory tells us that trade leads to growth in income. The question to be asked is: are the results equally allocated? Figure 3.10 on page 64 suggests that they are not. Despite the fact that the developing world received $54 billion of aid in 1990, their unequal position in world trade cost them $500 billion. If trade took place in a free market, where people, goods and money had ready access to every country, greater equality between countries would result.

This creates a serious dilemma for many countries, because breaking into world markets can appear to be the only way to make the leap into the rich world. The newly industrialised economies of the Pacific Rim

Figure 3.10 Cost of global markets to developing countries

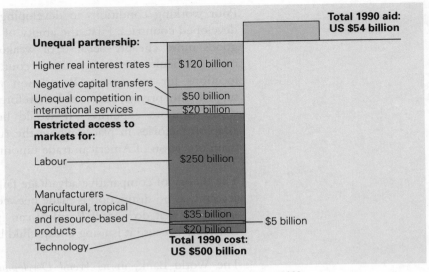

Source: *Human Development Report*, UN Development Program, 1992

bear witness to the success of this strategy, which others seek to emulate. Few countries have succeeded in making such a rapid transition and it seems improbable that it is a route that all can take. In these countries, which have used the trade route to swift development, the distribution of income has shifted from the pattern of pre-industrial countries, in which the lowest and highest percentiles may have a larger share of national income than in many developed countries. As the economy grows, it adds to the income of the upper percentiles. Figure 3.11 shows the process under way in some Pacific Rim economies. Thailand and Malaysia, having developed further, show a larger share going to the top 20%. The UK is included for comparison.

Figure 3.11 Income distribution in industrialising economies

Country	Lowest 20%	Second quintile	Third quintile	Fourth quintile	Top 20%
Indonesia	8.7	12.1	15.9	21.1	42.3
Philippines	6.5	10.1	14.4	21.2	47.8
Thailand	6.1	9.4	13.5	20.3	50.7
Malaysia	4.6	8.3	13.0	20.4	53.7
UK	5.8	11.5	18.2	25.0	39.5

Source: World Bank, *World Development Report*, 1993

Lorenz curves

The pattern of poverty has also shifted. In a country that is predominantly agricultural, poverty will be mainly rural, but as industrialisation takes place many of these people will move to the growing urban areas. This may or may not offer improvement, as the data in Figure 3.12 demonstrate. Indonesia has more urban than rural poverty.

Figure 3.12 Poverty in industrialising economies

Country	Total	% of population Rural	Urban
Indonesia	17	16	20
Philippines	58	63	48
Thailand	32	34	15
Malaysia	32	38	13
Average for all developing countries	32	36	25

Source: *Human Development Report*, UN Development Program, 1993

Making trade more equitable

Urban poverty: slums on the outskirts of Jakarta, Indonesia.

Despite the negative effects of GATT mentioned earlier in this Enquiry, several aspects of its work were aimed at enhancing the position of many poor countries in relation to the rest of the world. The Multi-Fibre Arrangement, which permitted countries to limit the import of textiles, was set up to allow developed countries to adjust their own industries to cope with competition from cheaper producers. Little adjustment took place and the agreement finally lasted thirty years. The Uruguay Round began the process of liberalisation. In addition, developing countries with per capita GDP of less than $1,000 per year will be allowed to continue to subsidise exports. These small contributions show a willingness to assist some of the world's poorest countries. Relatively, however, the developed world still gained more than proportionately.

Attempts have been made by some organisations, both charitable and commercial, to use trade as a way of helping at a grass-roots level. Both Body Shop and Oxfam have, for example, set up commercial operations to assist in a very specific way. Body Shop has a 'Trade not aid' programme, which provides communities with the tools and resources they need to support themselves. Each project must be commercially viable for both parties.

Oxfam, with three other organisations, now imports, processes and sells Cafédirect, a brand of filter coffee. All have experience in working directly with the producers and realise the benefits of doing so. Small-scale coffee producers hit by the collapse of the International Coffee

Trade not aid

India

The Body Shop helped set up wood-turning workshops in Tamil Nadu, employing over 190 people to produce wooden massage rollers for the feet. A premium is paid by the Body Shop to a Community Action Fund, which has so far provided health care, education and improved working conditions.

Nepal

In 1988, The Body Shop set up a project in the Kathmandu Valley to produce hand-made paper products. As well as providing jobs for 67 people, the programme uses local organic materials and revives a traditional craft dating back from the eleventh century. 10% of the price we pay for the products goes into a Community Action Fund, which has so far underwritten education, healthcare, environmental and economic initiatives in the region.

Brazil

The Body Shop has forged links with the Kapayo Indians of the Amazon Basin. The Kapayo produce brazil nut oil from nuts they harvest from the rain forest. We use the oil in Brazil Nut Conditioner. They also make a traditional range of beaded wrist bands for sale in branches of Body Shop.

New Mexico

Blue corn grown and processed by the Pueblo Indians is the basis of our Blue Corn products, the first time we've produced a range specifically for one market (ie the USA). Responding to a specific market's need suggests exciting possibilities for new 'Trade not aid' projects.

Source: Body Shop, *Annual Report and Accounts 1993*

agreement have become vulnerable to poverty and exploitation. As coffee bushes take four years to mature, farmers cannot diversify readily. The coffee is imported from Mexico, Peru, Costa Rica and Nicaragua. The producers are indigenous people with small family farms generally working as co-operatives. The most important factor for the producers is that they receive almost four times as much for their coffee as they otherwise would. Profits for everyone else along the chain are slightly lower but several supermarkets have been prepared to stock Cafédirect.

Although these are very small initiatives, they demonstrate how producers in developing countries can be helped effectively. These two examples show how trade can be developed from a low base, while assisting communities to raise their standard of living. The case study of Tunisia, earlier in the Enquiry, showed the importance of human development as a stepping-stone to successful growth. The Body Shop and Cafédirect initiatives are helping small communities to make such changes.

The possibilities for future development of such small-scale, mutually beneficial trading arrangements depend not only on the willingness of companies in the developed world to become involved, but also on the willingness of consumers to pay a price a little over the odds for goods that are produced with equity in mind as well as efficiency.

Enquiry 4:   Is growth the solution?

Scope

The primary objective of both trade and aid is to assist in the growth of an economy. This can, but does not always, lead to a more equal distribution of income. This enquiry investigates the outcomes of growth and seeks the circumstances that lead to greater equality.

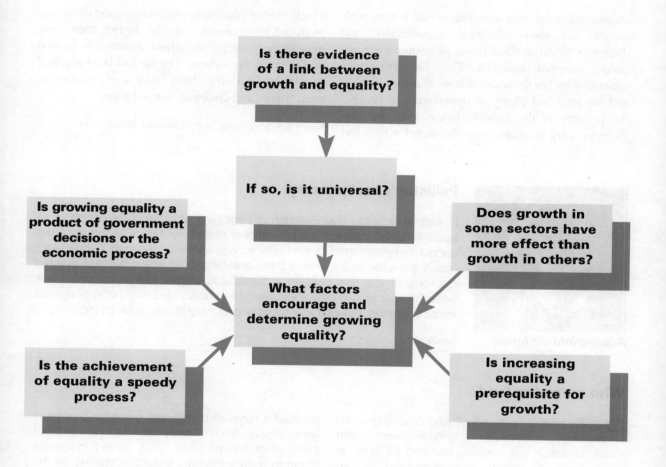

Opening evidence

Debt relief cannot wait

GROWTH in Africa continues to stagnate, the debt burden is rising and the chance of the region's creditors, now mainly individual governments, receiving repayments is receding. Sub-Saharan Africa's debt stock has risen from some £60bn in 1980 to over $183bn today, more than the value of the region's gross domestic products. Servicing this debt now consumes 25 per cent of sub Saharan Africa's export earnings, far higher than in any other region.

This debt service imposes an intolerable burden on many African economies, sucking abroad resources which should be being invested at home. And that is only part of the problem. Debt relief has become Africa's obsession.

Source: *Financial Times*, 28 September 1993

Education, organisation and discipline

Development does not start with goods; it starts with people and their education, organisation, and discipline. Without these three, all resources remain latent, untapped, potential. There are prosperous societies with but the scantiest basis of natural wealth, and we have had plenty of opportunity to observe the primacy of the invisible factors after the war. Every country, no matter how devastated, which had a high level of education, organisation, and discipline, produced an 'economic miracle'. In fact, these were miracles only for people whose attention is focused on the tip of the iceberg. The tip had been smashed to pieces, but the base, which is education, organisation, and discipline, was still there.

Source: E.F. Schumacher, *Small is Beautiful*, Abacus, 1974

Pakistan's real poverty

Reading into the future.

IT seems possible that Pakistan is beginning to redress the worst of its social wrongs: a disastrous educational record. Its failure in this area has undoubtedly damaged its economy as well as the hopes of its people. As a report last year by the World Bank analysing East Asia's success pointed out, one of the few policies successful countries had in common was heavy investment in education. Pakistan shows up badly not just against those countries, but also against its poorer neighbours, such as India.

Source: *The Economist*, 5 March 1994

Who owns the land?

POOR people are edgy about losing their property because urbanisation and industrialisation are creating demand for land, in a country in which land-ownership is an extremely murky business. Only 7% of the land on the Indonesian archipelago has a clear owner. In much of the Indonesian countryside, villagers practise a form of communal ownership or pass land down from family to family, without the use of formal titles. That leaves Indonesia trying to build a modern, industrial society on the basis of pre-industrial patterns of land ownership.

Source: *The Economist*, 5 March 1994

Large companies – small economies

Companies and countries	Sales/GDP ($m)
General Motors	132,774
Indonesia	116,476
Argentina	114,344
Saudi Arabia	108,640
Exxon	103,547
Ford Motor	100,785
Royal Dutch Shell	98,935
Turkey	95,763
Thailand	93,310
Toyota Motor	79,114
Poland	78,031
Hong Kong	67,555
IRI	67,547
Portugal	65,103
IBM	65,099
Daimler Benz	63,339
Israel	62,687
General Electric	62,202
Hitachi	61,645
BP	58,215
Greece	57,900
Matsushita	57,480
Mobil	57,388
Volkswagen	56,734
Venezuela	53,440
Siemens	51,401
Nissan	50,247
Peru	48,366
Fiat	47,928
Philippines	44,908
Unilever	43,962
New Zealand	42,861

Source: *Fortune*, 26 June 1993; World Bank, *World Development Report*, 1993

A many headed monster

Hunger is a many headed monster. The undernutrition that haunts a large part of humanity relates to a wide range of deprivations. The connections between different types of deprivation are not only biological but also economic and social. The idea of 'social security' is that of using social means to prevent deprivation and vulnerability. Social means can be of various types. Perhaps the most immediate is to provide direct support to the ability of the vulnerable to acquire the means to basic capabilities. Providing free food or cash to a potential famine victim is an obvious example of this. On a more regular basis providing unemployment insurance, free health services and basic education are other examples of such direct support. The social means could also be indirect. For example creating the social conditions of economic growth may make a substantial – and lasting – contribution to eliminating deprivation, if growth involves widespread participation of the population in the process of economic expansion.

Source: Jean Dreze and Amartya Sen, *Hunger and Public Action*, Clarendon Paperbacks, 1989

Granddad, what was it like to have a job?

MOST people throughout human history have lived lives combining back-breaking labour with frequent under-employment. The irony is that before industrialisation, starting at the end of the 18th century, most people wanted less leisure and more work – just to survive.

Two hundred years on, technological progress has brought to western Europe and north America at least the reality that a large and growing proportion of people do not work, and do not seem to need to. At least, at the moment, Western economies seem able to pay for 10–15 per cent chronic unemployment plus a steadily growing number of retired people.

Twenty years ago, economists and their fellow futurologists confidently expected that scientific developments would mean more leisure for all, as labour-saving devices cut the working week and still increased production. The age of Aquarius was to be brought about by science.

Today, the cruel reality has dawned. Whole professions have been rendered redundant by computerisation and the robot.

Source: *The European*, 16 September 1993

GNP and poverty

We were taught to take care of our GNP as this will take care of our poverty. Let us reverse this and take care of our poverty as this will take care of the GNP.

Source: Mahbub ul Haq, 'Employment and income distribution in the 1970s: a new perspective', *Development Digest*, October 1971

1 Growth and the individual

A diverse picture

Production possibility frontier

Growth means an increase in a country's real GDP. Although there is a general upward trend in the amount that is produced, growth rates vary greatly throughout the world. Figure 4.1 shows a range of countries from the very rich to the very poor and demonstrates the degree of variation within and between groups. Countries with negative growth rates can be found in all categories, apart from the high-income group. Some low-income countries start from such a low threshold that the introduction of a new industry or the improvement in techniques used in an existing one can have a significant effect on the output figures. In the countries that are achieving growth, the size of the cake is increasing but does this mean that everyone's slice is getting larger?

Figure 4.1 Average growth rates of GNP

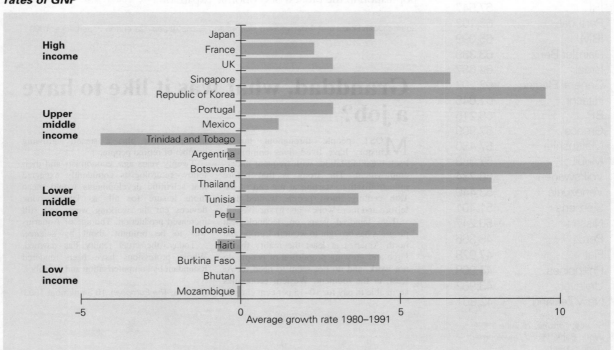

Average growth rate 1980–1991

Source: World Bank, *World Development Report*, 1993

Growth will not necessarily affect the lifestyles of all the residents of a country. During the 1980s, the UK achieved relatively high growth rates, in European terms, but this was not reflected in the incomes of some sectors of the population. Figure 4.2 analyses the changing pattern of income distribution in this period. By the end of the decade, the lowest quintile received a smaller proportion of total income than at the beginning of this period, whereas the top quintile had gained substantially.

Figure 4.2 Income distribution in the UK

| Net income after housing costs | Quintile groups % | | | | | |
	Bottom fifth	Next fifth	Middle fifth	Next fifth	Top fifth	Total
1979	9.6	14.1	18.1	23.1	35.3	100.0
1981	9.0	13.6	17.8	23.1	36.5	100.0
1987	7.6	12.3	17.1	22.9	40.1	100.0
1988–1989	6.9	12.0	17.0	22.9	41.1	100.0

Source: CSO, *Social Trends*, 1993

Taxes and benefits

In the UK this change in distribution was, in part, a result of government policy. The market was being used to drive the economy, so taxes and benefits were being cut in order to motivate people to be more productive. This demonstrates how the government can be influential in affecting the proportion of income received by different sectors. With alternative taxation policies the pattern might be reversed. During the period shown in Figure 4.2, the growing GDP meant that even the bottom quintile was not worse off in real, absolute, terms but the gains at the top end were, therefore, even more significant.

A trend to equality?

The pattern of income distribution tends to be more equal in developed countries than in the rest. One of the key factors that accounts for this has already been raised in the context of the UK. The greater inequality that emerged in the 1980s was explained by changing government policies, which suggests that a system exists that enables a proportion of income to be transferred from the rich to the poor. Taxation and benefits are taken for granted in the developed world, but in many developing countries there are either no such systems or very embryonic ones. The level of social infrastructure also affects equality. The number of hospitals, the levels of education and life expectancy will all contribute to a picture of the quality of life of individuals in a country.

The graph in Figure 4.3 on page 72 shows a best-fit line for the proportion of health spending that is met by the government. The group that falls into the top right hand corner is composed of the most highly developed countries, where the government takes a high level of responsibility for the healthcare of the population. The two exceptions to this are Hong Kong and the USA, where the private sector dominates through insurance schemes.

As the line moves towards the origin it falls rapidly, showing that governments in the poorest countries make very little contribution to healthcare. It is often available for the sectors of the population who can pay the market price, but scarcely exists for others. Such factors exaggerate the differentials shown by the statistical measures of income inequality.

Figure 4.3 The public share of total health spending

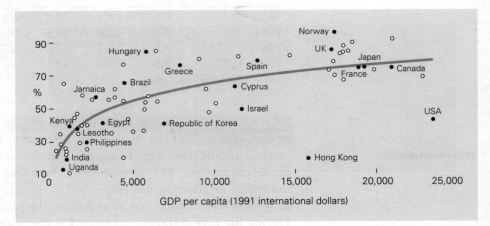

Source: World Bank, *World Development Report*, 1993

In Figure 4.4, the effects of this disparity are shown. Some of the countries on the scatter graph have been labelled in order to show that the relationship between life expectancy and the level of development is quite apparent. The differentials are great, but much progress has been made in the second half of the twentieth century, when the gap between rich and poor has narrowed slightly in some areas and more substantially in others. Sub-Saharan Africa, India and Asia have shown a relatively smaller gain than the rest of the developing world.

Figure 4.4 Life expectancy and GNP

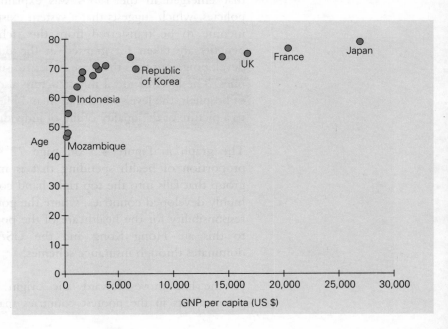

Source: World Bank, *World Development Report*, 1993

Although it is generally true that developed countries have a more equitable distribution of income, the pattern does not show as clearly when comparisons are made within groups. Among low-income countries there is a wide range of income distribution patterns. The following examples demonstrate this and identify some of the issues that are central to the process of development. These are discussed later on in this enquiry.

India

relying on experiment & observation rather than theory

India has been a centre of significant economic growth in recent years, but rural poverty still exists. Official data suggests that incomes are becoming more evenly distributed but empirical evidence questions this. The proportion of the population living in rural poverty has fallen from 51% in the 1970s to 28% by 1990. This, however, disguises the fact that as the country has industrialised, rural economies have grown less rapidly while supporting an increasing number of people. Rural incomes have been left behind, as non-agricultural incomes have risen to three times their level. The process of industrialisation has failed to utilise enough of the labour force to absorb the surplus that has been created in rural communities. The number of people involved in casual labour has increased, as agriculture has found them surplus to requirements and the industrial sector has not been able to occupy them. A further factor which suggests that inequality persists on a large scale is that the growth in consumption has come from consumer durables. Such products are beyond the scope of most of the rural communities, whose consumption of foodgrains has actually fallen, with the result that almost one-half of the population is under-nourished.

The income disparities in the data for the regions reinforces the picture. The richest state in the country produces nearly six times the per capita output of the poorest and this is reflected in the distribution of rural poor and the figures for household expenditure.

There appears to be a relationship between the growth of labour productivity and the prosperity of a region. Where labour productivity is growing relatively quickly, there seems to be less poverty. In agricultural areas, where growth has been, on average, only 0.65% per annum, there is a higher proportion of the population in poverty. The Green Revolution, which introduced new farming methods and higher yielding grain crops, certainly increased yields, but the benefits do not appear to have reached all the rural population. Future development of new strains of cereals which can improve yields in the arid regions may assist. But more open government and a free press are important factors in raising awareness of the problems associated with poverty and therefore increasing pressure to help the rural poor.

In order to escape rural deprivation, many people move to the towns and cities in search of a better way of life. Their destination often has less to offer than they anticipated. Although the data for urban poor suggests that the proportion is declining, the movement to the cities has increased the absolute numbers so that many more people are living in poverty. The conditions in which they live are squalid because the urban infrastructure has been unable to cope with the growth of the cities and their populations. The unskilled find work hardest to come by, so they are the most likely to find themselves without financial support.

To separate into opposed groups etc.

At present, the population of India appears to be <u>polarising</u>. Those who are in the dynamic growth industries are moving into a society that reflects the developed world. Televisions, cars and other consumer durables are becoming commonplace in many urban homes. The other sector of society, which has its roots in the rural community, has failed to move ahead at the same rate and may even have slipped backwards.

The Republic of Korea

Figure 4.5 The growth of Korea

Year	Annual average growth rate
1950–60	3.0%
1960–70	5.6%
1970–80	7.2%
1980–90	8.7%

Source: World Bank

The Republic of Korea, or South Korea, as it is commonly called, has shown a startling rate of growth, as shown in Figure 4.5. In the second half of the twentieth century it has grown at an average of 8% a year, which is twice the rate of other, less developed countries. While achieving this, it has also succeeded in improving living standards for its population. It has a Gini co-efficient of 0.36 and a relatively small proportion – 13% – of its population are classified as living in poverty. Life expectancy has risen from 55 in 1960 to 71 in 1990 and infant mortality has fallen from 62 to 17. The country spends 6.4% of GNP on healthcare.

In education, it has outstripped many other countries in the upper middle-income category. All children attend primary school and approximately 85% of both boys and girls go through secondary education. In 1965 only 35% of children and 25% of girls were educated beyond the elementary stage. In the UK in 1990 24% of the age-group were in tertiary education, whereas in South Korea the figure was 38%. As 22.4% of the country's public spending goes on education, it is obviously regarded as important. There are, however, still inequalities in housing and social conditions for a country with a relatively high average income.

Human capital

Government planning

South Korea has for many years had high levels of saving and investment. Also, the government has had a strong role in its country's dramatic growth. Imports have been limited to those that are important for export production, and export industries have been given assistance and targets have been set for production. The country has been export-oriented from the beginning of its development phase in the 1960s, thus encouraging this rapid growth to take place in its manufacturing industry. A powerful, militarised government has enabled decisions to be put into practice that might not have been possible under more liberal conditions.

The modern city of Seoul, South Korea, reflects the country's rapid growth.

Open Question

Does economic growth compensate for authoritarian government?

The country is slowly becoming more democratic, but is still very authoritarian. This results, to a large extent, from the uneasy frontier with the Democratic Republic of Korea, or North Korea, where American troops are still stationed.

Brazil

Brazil's growth-rate was rapid in the late 1960s and early 1970s, when it reached 10% a year, of which manufacturing was the dominant feature. It first produced for the home market, but as world trade expanded the focus was changed, thus providing wider opportunities. In the 1980s, however, the growth rate fell to 2.9%

Unlike in South Korea, however, the industrialisation process has been accompanied by growing disparity in individuals' income and welfare. Brazil's Gini co-efficient is 0.57, which is high for a country at any stage of development. There are now 39% of children in secondary education, compared to 16% in 1965. Spending on education has risen to 17.7% of total public expenditure, but this has not yet permeated the system. Infant mortality is 57 per thousand live births and life expectancy is 66. Brazil spends 3.9% of GNP on healthcare.

In the late 1970s and early 1980s Brazil's military government became increasingly unpopular and since then the country has gradually become more democratic. This has not led to an improvement in social policies, partly because of the huge external debts that have built up. In the 1980s, the threat of the country defaulting on its $10 billion debt caused the IMF to lend the country even more so that it could pay the interest on existing debt. By 1990 the figure still stood at $116,173 million.

2 The labour issue

Does growth mean more jobs?

India faces a situation in which increased industrialisation does not lead to increased demand for labour. This is a pattern that is being repeated throughout the world in both developed and developing countries. In some European countries, despite relatively strong growth, unemployment has been growing. In 1991 there were 30 million unemployed in the OECD countries. Three-quarters of the rise in output has come from increased productivity, and the other quarter has been generated by capital investment. Figure 4.6 shows the disparity between economic growth and the growth of employment in the major regions of the world.

Productivity

The drive for productivity and the relatively high price of labour in industrialised countries encourage the development of capital-intensive machinery. Despite the fact that developing countries have low labour costs, it is this type of new equipment that is often installed as it is needed to produce the consumer goods the world market seeks. This is reflected by the fact that less than one-third of the increase in output in developing countries came from an increase in employment, and more than two-thirds resulted from investment in machinery.

Capital-intensive investment

Transnational corporations bring large investments to some developing countries but involve relatively few people. It is estimated that the total transnational employment in these countries is 7 million – about 1% of the total workforce. About a further 1% are involved in businesses that supply these large companies. The proportion of the workforce employed by transnationals appears to be falling.

Populations in the developing world are likely to continue to grow at the existing rate of 2.3% per year throughout the 1990s, which means that 260 million new jobs will be needed to absorb the increase. Combined with the increasing number of women joining the workforce and the migration to cities, approximately 1 billion new jobs will be required before the end of the century. In the 1980s the number of jobs grew at a rate of 3% a year. To meet the growth in population, 4% job growth is currently needed.

The number of jobs is not the only issue. The quality of jobs is also declining. Again, in both the developed and developing worlds people are becoming less secure. The growth of casual labour in India has been referred to, and this pattern is reflected in many countries. A small number of highly skilled people form the core of the labour force; the rest are often on temporary and short-term contracts because small entrepreneurs are unwilling to commit themselves to a permanent arrangement when they are dependent on receiving orders from large organisations.

Figure 4.6 Jobless growth, 1975–2000

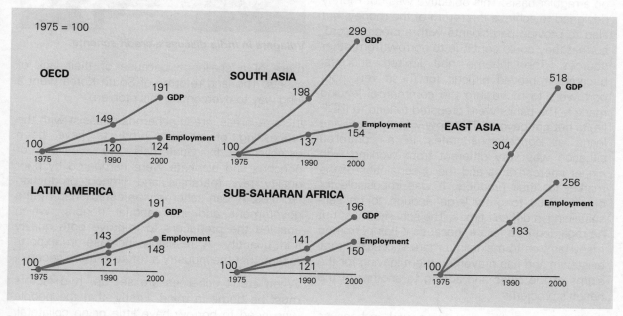

Source: *Human Development Report,* UN Development Program, 1993

Is entrepreneurship an answer?

An effective method of increasing employment is to encourage people to set up their own businesses. The developed world already demonstrates a growing trend towards self employment. The increasing number of business start-ups reflects this. In the developing world there are already many small-scale entrepreneurs, because of the predominance of agriculture. There is, however, a strong need for this to shift into the manufacturing and service sectors in order to assist in overcoming the growing trend towards unemployment.

Sources of finance

Credit has always been a problem for small organisations. The rural communities of India have been trapped in poverty because they have not had access to credit or assets that would enable them to develop the resources that they have. Commercial lenders are not prepared to offer finance to people with little or no collateral and no past record of repayment, unless it be at exorbitant interest rates.

India: the Integrated Rural Development Plan

The IRDP was established to help overcome the problems of rural unemployment by providing state-subsidised loans and assets to poor landless farmers. An important element of the policy of the IRDP was that borrowers should be able to run a viable, self-supporting enterprise, which would enable them to pay back their loans on a regular basis. This objective was not merely designed to achieve the return of the money, but also to provide participants with a credit record, so that they could continue to borrow from other sources. The scheme had limited success, because it proved difficult for these very poor borrowers to move into the commercial lending market. The banks were prepared to lend to IRDP limits but not beyond. The view was that repaying loans at concessional rates in a controlled situation was very different from working with higher interest rates and the uncertainties of the market for their products. It was impossible for organisations to grow large enough to be self-sustaining in difficult times. The scheme must not be regarded as a failure, because it has permitted many families to maintain a more successful rural existence and has prevented them leaving for the slums of the cities and adding to another of the nation's problems

Agriculture is a difficult area to work in because of the instability of prices and the general decline in the primary product market. The landless rural poor, who the IRDP was trying to help, are even

Villagers in India discuss a credit scheme.

more of a challenge because of their lack of assets. The land reforms of South Korea went a long way to overcoming this problem.

In some areas, credit schemes to assist with the processing of primary products have been established. In Guatemala the weavers of ponchos and blankets were hampered by poor quality raw materials and limited production facilities. A loan scheme was established by the government and international donors, which enabled the producers to improve both quality and quantity. A resulting increase in exports means that the industry's future is more secure.

When credit schemes are set up, two factors must be borne in mind. Firstly, that the people who need to borrow have little or no collateral, and secondly, access must be given to weaker groups through co-operatives, savings groups and credit unions.

Many people who run small enterprises lack training in how to run a business. The provision of courses or more individual assistance would help more small firms to survive.

The nature of government

Both Korea and Brazil developed rapidly when under the control of extremely authoritarian governments. One has developed a structure in which the population has healthcare and education plus an income distribution that is relatively equitable. The other has a highly inequitable economic system. It appears that the policies of the government are more important than the political structure of the country when the achievement of growth is the objective. The Human Development Index, which the

United Nations Development Programme constructs to compare the quality of life as well as national income, places South Korea thirty-third out of a total of 173 countries in the world. Brazil is seventieth.

The move towards democracy and concern for human rights raises questions about development at all costs. Despite South Korea's good record of social and economic indicators, the authoritarian state has been an extremely dominant force in the country and has been subject to protest for the last decade.

If individuals are to have more control over the political life of their country, government must come closer to them. Decentralisation, in which power is passed to the regions and local authorities, gives people greater power. It also allows revenue to be raised at a local level, which again gives people the power to make decisions about their own locality.

Decentralisation has its costs and benefits. It can be more efficient, because projects are carried out in a way that is appropriate for the region. For example, a bridge-building scheme in Nepal, which used local labour and materials, cost a quarter of the central government plan.

On the other hand, regions may not have the expertise or the government's ability to maintain standards, as is demonstrated by local schools in an area of Kenya. Only 13% of their students reach the minimum standard that is attained by 80% of those in government schools. The regions may also lose economies of scale when trying to match investment to small communities.

By decentralising, people are empowered within their region, and equity generally increases. But on a national level regional inequalities may become more apparent. Rich areas tend to be more powerful and are, therefore, able to attract a greater share of the national cake. This increases an existing inequality. In Mexico, for example, the cities and tourist areas have received a higher than proportionate share of the healthcare budget, which left the rural Indians relatively worse off.

Provided that these factors are taken into account, decentralisation can assist in increasing employment, because local expenditure can provide the structures that are necessary. Even small-scale industry cannot develop without adequate infrastructure. Local authorities should be better placed to make decisions about the provision of water, electricity and roads. They are more likely to be well maintained on a local basis, where their importance is recognised. The need for support for local entrepreneurs will also be appreciated, so the provision of credit schemes and training may be more effectively organised.

It is extremely difficult to assess the economic effects of decentralisation, because growth comes as the result of so many varied factors that it is hard to pin down a specific relationship. There are as many examples of situations where decentralisation has been effective as ones where it has not, but the reason for the success or failure is not always clear.

3 The transnational corporation: a spur to growth?

The incentives

The transnational corporation has been a source of controversy in the development debate. Does it help or hinder the economic growth of a country?

In a highly competitive world market, companies are seeking locations where they can establish plants that will give them a cutting edge in pricing their products. Many governments found the prospects of factories being set up by large overseas companies appealing. They would provide employment and, it was hoped, help to move the economy higher in the growth league tables.

Figure 4.7 shows some of the tax incentives offered to foreign investors in Singapore.

Figure 4.7 Tax incentives for investors in Singapore

1 'Pioneer' status for approved manufacturing and service activities – exemption from tax on profits for five to ten years.

2 Expansion incentive for approved manufacturing and service activities – exemption from tax on profits for five years.

3 Export incentives on approved export activities – 90% tax concessions on profits.

4 Double tax deduction for expenses on export promotion and development.

5 Double tax deduction for expenses on research and development.

6 Accelerated depreciation allowance.

7 Tax exemption on income from Singapore registered ships.

8 Tax concession of 50% on export income from approved warehousing, technical or engineering services, or consultancy services, or international trading companies.

Singapore's policy worked very effectively. By the mid 1980s foreign firms were responsible for 70% of gross output in the manufacturing sector, employed more than 50% of the workforce and generated 82% of direct exports. In fact more than 25% of Singapore's GDP was produced by foreign companies.

The case for TNCs

The arguments in favour of foreign investment are very similar to the ones for foreign aid. It helps to fill the gaps that a developing economy cannot meet:

- The generation of saving is generally inadequate to permit large-scale industrial investment, so the introduction of finance from elsewhere allows it to go ahead. By doing so, the economy will grow and generate further income, so the multiplier effect of such an injection is to be welcomed.
- The country will receive the benefit of the latest technology, which it could not afford from its own resources.
- By bringing in firms that want to produce goods for export, the balance of payments will benefit. Despite the additional imports of capital goods and raw materials, there should be a net gain.
- The country will probably have an inadequate supply of appropriate skilled personnel to staff a modern plant, so the introduction of overseas staff will provide the basis for training a future workforce. Not only will technical experts be installed, but managerial staff will be brought in as well. Their duty will be to train the local employees in coping with the complexities of decision making and dealing with international markets.
- The foreign companies will add to the country's tax revenue and therefore assist in the provision of funds for developing new infrastructure and the provision of other facilities, which will help in improving the quality of life for the resident population.

The interests of transnationals may have much in common with the interests of the country where they have set up companies. The case study of Hindustan Lever Ltd demonstrates how investment that helped the company to run more efficiently also helped the local community to become more productive and improve its standard of living. Where benefits are mutual, there is more security for both parties because a dependency culture does not develop.

The Integrated Rural Development Programme

The dairy products factory that Hindustan Lever Ltd (HLL) had set up in the Etah district of Uttah Pradesh consistently failed to achieve its targets. The factory was running at only 50% of capacity, mainly because of an inadequate supply of milk. The company's first instinct was to sell the factory, but the state government intervened and HLL was persuaded to continue with the venture.

There was a growing realisation that the future of the factory was

Efficiency

inextricably linked with the socio-economic development of the area. By improving agricultural practices, the farmers would benefit because their incomes would rise. Their increased output would also secure a reliable supply of milk, so the company could run more efficiently.

In order to achieve these ends, an integrated programme was established, which aimed to educate farmers in more efficient methods while developing strategies to assist villagers with the improvement of sanitation, health and education. Etah had some of the lowest agricultural yields in all of India, so the first need was to discover the problems that confronted the farmers. Local supervisors from the factory were sent to live in five villages for a period of six weeks to investigate. They identified the following sources of difficulty:

- *A lack of finance.* The local money-lenders charged high interest rates and the banks would not lend for fear of default.

- *A lack of agricultural expertise.* Both animal husbandry and crop-yields suffered because local farmers received no advice.

- *A lack of reliable supplies of inputs.* Seeds, fertilisers, pesticides and equipment could not be obtained easily.

- *Lack of warehousing and marketing facilities.* Output had to be sold when produced because of lack of storage facilities.

The five supervisors became responsible for the development of Integrated Rural Development (IRD) in the villages that they had surveyed. Farmers, who were selected on the basis of their willingness to take advice, were given assistance with effective crop and livestock farming. Their farms become demonstration plots, which showed others the benefits of the scientific techniques. New crops and types of grain as well as new, more productive breeds of cow were introduced. The support provided enabled the farmers to apply for bank loans and government grants more effectively and then use the finance efficiently.

Productivity

At the end of the first year, the scheme was extended to take in a larger area. Reclamation of saline land was introduced and the villagers were provided with preventive healthcare while training was given in paramedical activities. This all took place approximately twenty years ago. The IRD has expanded from six villages to over thirty, and is still growing. Within five years of being introduced to the programme most villages have become self-supporting and could function within the system, so direct help could be withdrawn.

Major expansion of the dairy products factory is in hand. Milk collection will rise from 47,000 tonnes to 70,000 tonnes and sales are expected to increase accordingly, from 6,550 to 11,700 tonnes. Both gross capital employed and profits are expected to double.

The case against TNCs

The following points support the argument that transnationals do more harm than good:

1 The introduction of transnationals may reduce the savings and investment that would have taken place in their absence. To receive the incentives for a new project in Singapore, for example, the value of the investment had to be greater than $1 million. This immediately excluded most local enterprise because the figure was too high. Although a package was introduced for small firms, it did not come until 15 years after the one described in Figure 4.7.

2 Local businesses felt that they had suffered because the transnationals could bring in products with famous brand-names and sell them as loss-leaders in order to capture the market. This also discouraged local investment.

3 Importing the latest technology may have little effect on the local population. In fact it may undermine existing companies, which are trying to compete with less sophisticated equipment.

4 The balance of payments has been known to suffer in countries where transnationals have been established. Capital goods are imported to set up the new plants. Semi-finished goods may also be imported to be assembled and profits and other funds are remitted to the country of origin.

5 There may be little need to train the local workforce if the company brings in the experts that are required. The jobs carried out by the country's nationals tend to be low-skilled, and local initiatives may be thwarted by foreign dominance of the market.

6 As these companies receive substantial tax breaks, their contribution to the country's revenue is less than might be expected. Long established companies often continue to negotiate special terms in order to maintain their position.

7 The companies use their economic power to influence decisions that are taken by the government. They can play one country off against another to gain the best package of concessions and incentives.

8 Transnationals can use their power to influence political decision making at all levels, even to the extent of subverting the democratic system.

9 Their activities can create more inequalities by:

■ encouraging the development of a dual economy;
■ installing capital-intensive equipment, which employs a few specialist workers and offers little to the bulk of the population;
■ producing goods for the rich.

Costs of production

These factors suggest that a transnational company can be in an extremely powerful position in a developing country. The growth that results from their presence, however, generally increasing the demand for labour and causing wages to rise, is the _antithesis_ of the original attraction. So there is always the temptation to move the next development to another country, where wage levels are still low. The following extract sums up the situation in which Singapore found itself when it attempted to sell the country as a higher-skilled and therefore higher-waged economy.

a contrast of thoughts.

Singapore: infrastructure or cheap labour?

The Economic Development Board explained that they had misunderstood why companies had come to Singapore. Good infrastructure was important but it wasn't the main driver. Cheap wages were. Transnational companies, faced with the decree, didn't see the point of giving two-dollar-an-hour pay checks to unskilled Singaporeans when Malaysians, Thai or even Mexican workers could do the same job for under one dollar. On top of all that, all these countries had begun offering their own incentives to lure industry. So the Singapore shortcut was backfiring. Companies being courted, went elsewhere. Some already stopped investing. And a few got ready to pull out.

Source: Ira Magaziner and Mark Patinkin, *The Silent War: Inside the Global Business Battles Shaping America's Future*, Random House, 1989

It must be remembered, however, that Singapore continued to grow at an average of 6.6% a year throughout the 1980s, has a healthy balance of payments surplus and is now classified by the World Bank, with OECD countries, as a high–income economy. It has a Gini co–efficient of 0.42 and comes forty–third in the Human Development Index.

Open Question

Why do developing countries wish to attract transnationals?

The debate about transnationals is deeply political. Countries are keen to attract them, despite the inevitable conflict of interests. Why? The following article shows how a country responds to the fear of transnationals, or their sub–contractors, moving out.

Doing it, earning it.

THE components of the American dream are manufactured in small towns such as Serang in west Java. Warehouse-like factories, dotted among the rice fields, churn out fashionable athletic shoes for joggers and tennis players in the West. At one South Korean firm hundreds of women crouch over sewing machines making basket-ball shoes which will be sold in the high streets of the developed world. The women need all the encouragement they can get. Even after a recent 40% pay rise, most are paid less than $10 for a five-day week.

With many new entrants to the labour force each year, there is no shortage of Indonesians willing to work for so little. Indeed the transformation of former villages into workshops for the West is fundamental to Indonesia's economic strategy and to its hope of keeping its people employed.

The Indonesian government wants to keep costs down, but is also keen to contain labour unrest and meet the rising expectations of workers. The government has reacted to recent strikes with a mixture of iron fist and velvet glove. It recently increased the minimum wage in west Java to 3,800 rupiah ($1.80) a day and is threatening to prosecute factory owners who fail to meet their obligations. But at the same time the government is cracking down on the new, independent trade union, which is pushing for a further increase in the minimum wage to 7,000 rupiah a day. The union's attempt to organise a national one-hour strike was largely thwarted by the government's decision to detain the organisers for a short time.

Many western economists and businessmen in Jakarta are aghast at the government's heavy handed attitude to the new union; yet some also feel that even the minimum wage may be excessive. 'Those wages sound pitiful,' frets one economist, 'but they can't afford to increase wages faster than productivity. That would send the wrong signal to foreign investors.'

The foreign bosses say they will pay the new wages, but they are not happy about it. 'Wages go up,' complains the manager of the Korean-owned factory, 'but the buyers still try to force the costs down.'

The South Korean footwear companies in Indonesia know all about rising costs. In the past decade many have moved their factories to Indonesia or China because of rising wages and union militancy at home. Some fear that the footloose shoe companies could soon be on their way again. The lifting of the American trade embargo on Vietnam and economic reform in India and Bangladesh have opened up new and hungrier sources of cheap labour, which might yet interest the likes of Nike and Reebok. There are already some warning signals. New applications for foreign investment in Indonesia have fallen recently and exports seem to be levelling off.

Yet there are ways out of this problem. According to Indonesia's manpower ministry, labour costs are only 9.8% of production costs of the average factory. Some of the other costs are unnecessary. An American manager points out that 'corruption and bureaucracy siphon off a lot of the money you could pay to workers.' Indonesia received some applause for its deregulation package in October. But if it wants its workers to be better paid, the government needs to make a fresh assault on red-tape and under the table payments that are still a standard part of doing business in Indonesia.

Source: Adapted from *The Economist*, 26.February 1994

4 The debt trap

Why do countries borrow?

Circular flow

In order to develop, many countries borrowed from overseas sources. The level of savings within these countries was inadequate to supply the funds needed to allow industrialisation to take place. In low-income economies, consumers spend a high proportion, if not all, of their earnings to maintain a moderate standard of living. Only a small sector of the population receives an income large enough to allow them to save. In a developed economy, savings would be transmitted, via the banking system to individuals who sought to invest. Developing countries, therefore found the generation of sufficient funds for investment impossible.

In areas where money was available, the embryonic banking system was not adequate to channel the surplus to those who could use it for development. This is a common problem as countries industrialise. In the UK, the emergence of the banking system had allowed agricultural surpluses to be used to fund the Industrial Revolution of the late eighteenth century.

The process of industrialisation required the purchase of capital goods and expertise from overseas. Foreign exchange was needed to pay for these imports, but most countries found their supplies inadequate. As primary producers, they were experiencing a fall in the value of their exports, which compounded the problem, so borrowing became the only solution.

Borrowing was initially in the form of aid, with concessional rates of interest, for imports of capital goods and development projects. This was beneficial and repayments were under control. Then in the mid- to late-1970s and into the 1980s many governments borrowed at commercial rates from banks in the developed world. Initially interest rates were low. But when the developed country governments raised interest rates as part of their counter-inflation policy, the interest payments and repayments together created a burden that many borrowers proved unable to meet.

Open Question

What do debt-laden developing countries have to give up to meet the repayments?

To repay such debts, a country needs a strong currency, low interest rates and a good price for its exports. With commodity prices falling even further in the 1980s, commercial rather than concessional interest rates, and weak currencies, the major debtors had little chance of even paying the interest on their debts.

Brazil, which heads the list of major debtor countries, as shown in Figure 4.8, has found great difficulty in paying the debts, and the result is that a high proportion of government revenue is spent on meeting the payments. The opportunity cost is therefore substantial.

Figure 4.8 The major debtors, 1991

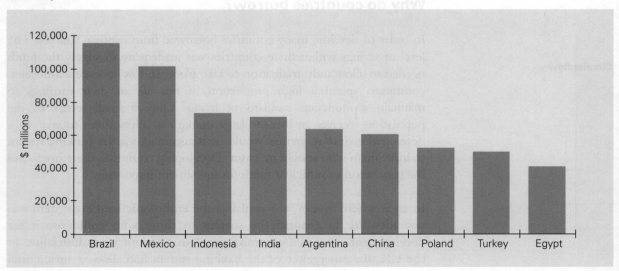

Source: World Bank, *World Development Report*, 1993

Why did it become a crisis?

In the 1970s commercial banks were competing to lend money to a small group of developing countries that were regarded as being reasonably stable. As a result, the lending was excessive and not on a sound financial basis. A herd instinct seemed to take over as the loans increased. In the banks' defence, the loans were being given to governments and in the past this has always meant that they were secure. Banks always charge higher rates of interest to customers with a lower credit rating, so these countries, which were not in the same category as the G7, for example, were expected to pay more than their counterparts in the developed world. This made the loans profitable for the banks.

The crunch came in 1982. Low levels of demand for exports, due to world-wide recession, and high interest rates, precipitated the problem. Mexico was the first country to announce that it was unable to pay the amounts that were due. This threw the entire banking system into panic and lending ceased altogether. This accentuated the problems for some countries, because they relied on the new loans to recycle the old ones.

The commercial debt was held by banks, which feared for their future if the repayments were not made. The Midland Bank, which held a higher proportion of such debt than the other big banks in the UK, found itself in an untenable position and was eventually sold to the Hong Kong and Shanghai Bank.

The whole debt issue is closely allied to the functioning of the world's financial systems, and fears were expressed that if a solution was not found the economies of the western countries could be seriously affected. Because of the potential impact on the world economy it was unthinkable that major commercial banks should be allowed to collapse, so they were supported by western governments. The developing countries had to resort to the IMF for assistance.

The nature of the investment that developing countries carried out on the strength of their borrowing did not help the situation. A commercial organisation that borrows money always ensures that the return on the investment will cover the interest payments and provide some profit. The debtor countries were generally using the funds to invest in projects to improve the infrastructure. Building a dam will provide water and electricity for the population and industry, but may not provide the return that is needed to pay off the debt. In the longer term, the improved facilities may encourage new industry to set up but this time-scale was too long for the lenders.

Strategies

Although the countries of sub–Saharan Africa do not appear among the major debtors in Figure 4.8, their problems are the most severe. They are absent from the graph because their economies are relatively small but their debts, as a group, are equivalent to 100% of GNP. Figure 4.9 lists several countries where debts exceed the total output of the country.

Repayment is an increasing problem, because they are mainly primary producers and, as has already been discussed, the value of their output has fallen steadily.

Figure 4.9 The ratio of debt to GDP

Country	$ millions 1991	
	GDP	Debt
Uganda	2,527	2,830
Madagascar	2,488	3,715
Mali	2,451	2,531
Nigeria	34,124	34,497
Zambia	3,831	7,279

Source: World Bank, *World Development Report,* 1993

The solutions to the debt problem all involve some difficulties. Any form of repayment has negative effects on the countries concerned, and it has been argued that it should be written off; but this has implications for the lenders. There is an understandable caution in letting go of these 'assets', which the banks and other institutions hold in the form of loans to the developing world.

The traditional way of coping with this problem is to reschedule the debt. This is done by delaying repayments or adding the unpaid interest to the capital sum. Both strategies make the problem worse in the long run, as the debt grows and increases the proportion of GDP that has to be spent on meeting the repayments. The economy can be put in jeopardy by these huge withdrawals of funds. They also have the effect of reducing potential government expenditure on services and facilities, which assist in the development process.

In order to reschedule their debts, countries have been asked to meet conditions that have been imposed by the IMF. Much criticism has been raised over this, because of their stringent terms and the resulting impact that they have had on developing economies.

The IMF's objective was to ease the repayment process and prevent countries from defaulting. To do this it was necessary to gain control of the economic situation. For example:

- *To reduce inflation:* Limit the amount of domestic credit expansion, thus reducing demand. This also assists with the next point.
- *To improve the balance of payments:* Devalue the exchange rate so imports become more expensive and exports become cheaper.
- *To reduce the government's control of the economy:* Reduce the budget deficit – which also curbs inflation and assists the balance of payments.

■ *To encourage market forces:* Remove subsidies – which also helps to cut the budget deficit.

All these conditions led in the short run to a contraction of the economy, which was the only solution if repayments were to be made in the foreseeable future.

A variety of strategies have been proposed over the years to overcome the problems. Small countries, for example, have been helped to buy back their debt to a ceiling of $10 million, at a proportion of its face value, with the support of the World Bank and some bilateral donors. Such schemes are not feasible on a larger scale, because of the size of the debts. The amount available would be a drop in the ocean for a country such as Nigeria, but has been of some help to smaller countries in sub-Saharan Africa.

Every plan that is devised can be looked at from the point of view of the lender and the borrower. The Brady Plan was the first proposal to be put forward that aimed to reduce the debts as well as rescheduling them. It was regarded as a success by the World Bank, which supported it with the IMF and Japan. Not everyone saw it in the same light, as the excerpt that describes its effect in the Philippines suggests.

The effect of debt repayment on the poor

The Philippines has a debt problem, which is nearly as severe as that of sub-Saharan Africa. Its GDP is $44,908 million and its debt is $31,879 million. The IMF assisted in the formulation of a 'Letter of Intent', which prescribed economic targets for the early 1990s. The strategy was an austerity package so that the government could pay back the new loan of £1.3 billion. Of this new money, £1.1 billion was to be used to pay off existing debt. To pay for the loan, taxes were to rise, utilities become more expensive, the subsidy on rice would disappear and government spending would fall.

Opportunity cost

The following case study identifies some of the effects.

Philippines: the impact of debt

According to a leading newspaper, not repaying the debt could save the life of one Filipino child every hour. This could be achieved by limiting the debt service to 20% of export earnings and allotting health its rightful share from savings realised in the national budget. This is indeed an emotionally powerful argument for a ceiling on debt servicing. But the Philippine congress has not approved a bill seeking to limit debt service, despite strenuous lobbying from the Freedom From Debt Coalition and other concerned groups.

Recent years have seen an inverse relationship between debt servicing and health spending in total national government expenditures. As debt service sharply increased (from 6.4% in 1965–72, to 17.1% in 1980–85 and finally to 42% in 1986–89), health expenditure steadily declined (from 5.2% in 1965–72 to 3.2% in 1986–89). Health was allocated only 3.3% of the 1990 budget, compared with 37% for debt servicing. On a per capita basis this budget for health works out as P120 (£2.50) for a year.

As a result of the IMF conditions set out in the Letter of Intent, the Department of Health even expects a sizeable reduction in its beneficiaries. This reduction means leaving 399,120 children denied milk and vitamins, 27,565 lepers deprived of treatment, 103,262 tuberculosis patients untreated and 16,100 schistosomiasis cases denied medicines.

Source: Rosalinda Pineda-Ofreneo, *The Philippines: Debt and Poverty*, Oxfam, 1991

The future

Some of the middle-income countries have successfully started to reduce their indebtedness, but other regions, particularly sub-Saharan Africa, face enormous structural adjustment if the problem is not overcome. Figure 4.10 shows the growing burden of debt shouldered by the developing countries.

Figure 4.10 Total debt: developing countries

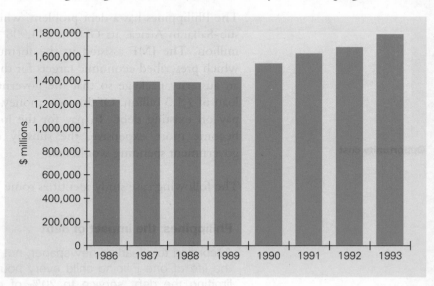

Source: *World Debt Tables*, 1993–94

The Trinidad proposals detailed below would be the best solution for these countries, but they have implications for others.

The Trinidad proposals

At a meeting of Commonwealth Finance Ministers in Trinidad in September 1990 modifications were proposed to the previously agreed 'Toronto terms' for bilateral debt reduction. The Toronto terms of 1988 had offered low-income, debt-distressed countries a series of options which included writing off one-third of their debts with various combinations of reduced interest rates and long repayment periods. The Trinidad modifications were:

- *Total debt:* instead of negotiating new terms as debts mature each year, the total debt of each country should be dealt with in one long-term operation

- *Debt write-off:* instead of one-third of the debt being written off, this should now be two-thirds. This would mean writing-off $18 billion of the debt stock of the poorest countries in Africa.

- *Repayment period:* this should be lengthened to twenty-five years.

- *Capitalisation:* interest payments due in the first five years should be capitalised. Principal and interest could then be repaid in a phased manner – increasing along with the debtor's capacity to repay

Source: *Human Development Report,* UN Development Program, 1992

None of these proposals is based on any firm estimates of the actual cost of, firstly, sorting out the debt crisis, and secondly, putting the countries back on a growth path that will not lead them to the same fate. A group of independent experts have developed a strategy which is based on past experience of debt repayment. It allows the countries to negotiate a package that is appropriate for their circumstances as is explained below.

Independent experts' proposals

The proposal was to establish a team of independent experts for each country. The team would be headed by a prominent person in finance, economics or political life. It would make proposals on debt reorganisation and the restoration of economic growth in the country concerned – as well as on the domestic measures needed to achieve this. The team's proposals would be put to debtors and creditors, who could then decide whether or not to accept them.

Such settlements would take time to agree and implement. So the group also proposed a series of interim bridging measures that, without prejudicing the outcome of the final settlement, could provide immediate relief to debtors. These include the postponement of amortisation and the payment of interest in three fractions:

1 to be paid as usual in foreign exchange
2 to be paid in local currency
3 to be capitalised into new loans

The size of each fraction would depend on the economic position of the debtor. These interim measures would not apply to concessional debt or to debts to creditors still making disbursements that exceed the cost of the debt service.

Source: *Human Development Report*, UN Development Program, 1992

Neither of these schemes achieves the World Bank's objective of a 'global bargain on debt' which will stop the annual transfer of $50 billion a year, in debt-related payments, from the South to the North. These, themselves, exacerbate the existing inequalities.

5 Growth and inequality

At the international level

As countries move along the continuum of growth, they progress through various stages of development. The largely agricultural society, where the majority of the population lives in rural communities, gives way to an increasingly urban structure, in which manufacturing industry grows to be dominant. The stage beyond this is identified by an increasing number of people working in service industries, while the manufacturing sector shrinks relatively. Throughout the process, there is generally a steady decline in the number of people involved in agriculture although output and productivity continue to increase.

The ends of the spectrum are moving steadily further apart as the countries at the developed end continue to grow at a steady pace and those at the bottom progress slowly, if at all. Many countries in between, particularly the newly industrialising economies, are rapidly shifting their position because of the speed of their development. The countries of the North have largely reached the latter stage, although some of the poorer countries of Europe are still on the fringes and have substantial sectors of their populations remaining dependent on agriculture.

This process is widening the gaps between rich and poor countries, although it does not always reflect the pattern of inequality between individuals.

Individuals in the long term

In a historical study of the effect that growth has on inequality, Professor Simon Kuznets, a Nobel Prize winner, came to the conclusion that there was a relationship between the two variables, which could be identified over a long period of time. It appears that in the early stages of development, income distribution becomes more unequal. The agricultural sector tends to be more equal than the rest of the economy. As growth tends to take place in the manufacturing sector, inequality rises in the early stages of development so the Gini co-efficient rises.

The problems of migration to the cities, where people often end up living in slums and shanty towns, often exacerbates poverty and inequality. At the other end of the scale, those who have jobs in the managerial levels of new industry will become wealthy in terms of the economy in which they live.

In the later stages of development, productivity increases tend to be more evenly spread across sectors, and the ownership of property becomes a less significant factor in household incomes. Countries also tend to develop tax and benefit systems that reduce inequality, thus reducing the Gini co-efficient.

In the developing world there is less evidence for this pattern. It may be too early to comment on the process for some economies, as forty or fifty years is a very short period when compared with the two centuries of development in the industrialised world.

As has been demonstrated in this enquiry, the pattern of income distribution differs significantly from one country to another. In the cases of South Korea and Brazil, the decisions made by governments had a strong impact on these outcomes. It is not the case that growth and equality are incompatible. The institutions and structures in each country will determine the outcomes.

The chicken or the egg?

There is little debate about the fact that growth can assist in the process of increasing equality and any programme that aims to overcome poverty will be looking for an increase in output to help in the achievement of its objectives. By increasing incomes, some can be made better off, without making others worse off. To turn this initial phase into self-sustainable growth, greater equality may be a prerequisite.

In countries where the pattern of distribution is very unequal, the poor have no surplus and therefore are unable to save. The rich often fail to invest their wealth in the development of the country, preferring an expensive lifestyle and depositing their money overseas. By equalising the distribution, more money will become available for saving and therefore investment.

A second benefit arises from this greater equality. As individuals' incomes rise, their demand for consumer goods also rises. This will stimulate the economy, provided that their purchases are home produced and not imported. The lower paid are more likely to increase their demand for locally produced food and clothing than are the rich, who can buy the expensive imports.

Improvements in living standards, health and education, which are a feature of a more equal distribution of income, also contribute to future growth. The workforce will become more productive and better able to adapt to new situations and therefore contribute to future development.

Enquiry 5:   Do solutions have their costs?

Scope

There are alternative strategies that can be used to overcome the problems of inequality identified in earlier enquiries. In this final section theses are investigated in a national, European and global context. The aim is to compare the outcomes and costs of policies that attempt to make the world a more equal place.

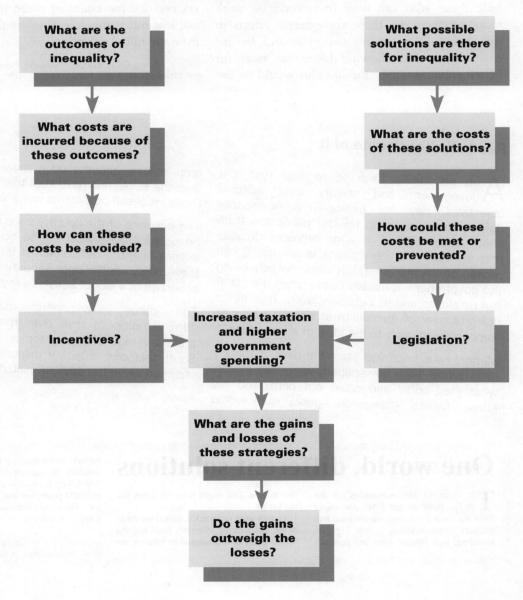

What are the outcomes of inequality?

What possible solutions are there for inequality?

What costs are incurred because of these outcomes?

What are the costs of these solutions?

How can these costs be avoided?

How could these costs be met or prevented?

Incentives?

Increased taxation and higher government spending?

Legislation?

What are the gains and losses of these strategies?

Do the gains outweigh the losses?

Opening evidence

Paying for inequality

In reality there are a number of policy areas in which positive sum outcomes can result from a redistribution of the resources of society. In these cases, the impact of the redistribution on the productive contributions of the poor leads to greater economic efficiency. This benefits not only those who can now find work, or work more productively: there are external effects in this case too as tax revenues rise and benefit expenditures fall, allowing lower tax rates (or better public services) for all. This would be the case where additional public expenditure on child care, or education, or training, or health for example reduces the economic exclusion of worse-off groups in society. The standard positive sum case would be where the benefits which flow from this greater economic participation (in tax revenue for example) mean that the rich do not lose out as much in absolute terms as appears from the initial redistribution.

Source: Andrew Glynn and David Miliband, *Paying for Inequality*, IPPS/Rivers Oram Press, 1994

Read all about some of it

ALL periodicals have to register with the government and specify their editorial objectives. Say, for example, a newspaper defines its aims as 'to tell the public the truth about public affairs'. If a government decides that an item in a newspaper is untrue, it can prosecute the publisher. If it wins – which, being the government, it usually does – then the paper can be closed and its publisher jailed. This, notes the professor of journalism at Korea University, 'is possibly contrary to the ideal of a free press.'

Matters have improved since the days of military rule. Before 1988 newspapers were told exactly what they could and could not print, and the Korean Central Intelligence Agency men would drop into newsrooms on a regular basis. Since then the KCIA men have kept their distance but a measure of self censorship remains.

The only one of the country's top newspapers to be persistently critical of the government is in severe financial difficulties. It is being sued by the Agency for National Security Planning for its coverage of a labour activist's mysterious death.

The other newspapers may take the administration to task over minor issues but their coverage of meaty topics, such as North-South relations or labour disputes, has scarcely changed since the days of military rule.

Source: *The Economist*, 25 September 1993

One world, different solutions

TO listen to the economists of the World Bank or the IMF, one might think the route to success was obvious: free markets, privatisation, low public spending, high interest rates and currency devaluation. This might work for some, but not for all.

Oxfam used last week's annual meetings of the International Monetary Fund and the World Bank in Washington to criticise the institutions for applying fashionable Western solutions to underdeveloped countries for which they are wholly inappropriate. Oxfam correctly points out that what might be right for Britain and France may be disastrous for China or Chad.

Source: Robert Chote in the *Independent on Sunday*, 26 September

Savage inequalities: other people's children

Four little boys are still asleep on the green rug an hour later when I leave the room. I stand at the door and look at the children, most of whom are sitting at a table now to have their milk. Nine years from now, most of these children will go on to Manley High School, an enormous, ugly building just a block away that has a graduation rate of only 38 per cent. Twelve years from now, by junior year of high school, if the neighbourhood statistics hold true for these children, 14 of these 23 boys and girls will have dropped out of school. Fourteen years from now, four of these kids, at most, will go to college. Eighteen years from now, one of those four may graduate from college, but three of the 12 boys in this kindergarten will already have spent time in prison.

* * * * * * *

Chicago, he tells me, does not have a junior high school system. Students begin school in kindergarten and remain here through eighth grade. Eighth grade graduation, here as elsewhere in Chicago, is regarded as a time for celebration, much as twelfth grade graduation would be celebrated in the suburbs. So there are parties, ball gowns and tuxedos, everything that other kids would have at high school graduation. 'For more than half our children,' says the principal, 'this is the last thing they will have to celebrate.'

Source: *NewsWeek* in *News Source*, 1992

'Poverty anywhere is a threat to prosperity everywhere'.

Source: *Human Development Report*, UN Development Program, 1993

Let's replace self-pity with self-reliance

THE current benefits system is both corrupt and corrupting, says David Marsland.

Every year, according to the prime minister's efficiency adviser, at least £5 billion – a tenth of the current deficit – is lost in benefits fraud. This 'revelation' should occasion anger, but none of the surprise with which it has been generally greeted. What else could reasonably be expected from a system which is corrupt and corrupting in its essential nature?

Since 1979, the government has begun to reform some sectors of the welfare system – in particular education, housing and health. Even if these initiatives are successful, however, partial reform leaves the underlying concept of the welfare state and the outmoded paternalistic values it enshrines entirely untouched.

What is needed is radical reform.

The early stages of state welfare provision in the period up to 1920 made some sort of limited sense given persisting poverty and social disruption. Even the elaboration and bureaucratic institutionalisation of the welfare state in the 1940s could be made to seem at least halfway plausible in the context of post-war reconstruction. Since then, however, standards of living and the quality of life of the whole population have been improved out of all recognition by straightforward economic progress. There ought to be far less need for welfare than in the past, and yet we consistently spend more and more on its provision.

Regardless of resourcing levels, the welfare state does not and cannot produce its intended outcomes. A large proportion of the taxes extracted expensively from the prosperous majority are recycled even more expensively to the same people. The streetwise majority cunningly syphon off still more of the assistance intended for the disadvantaged minority into their own pockets. Those who really need help very often don't get it, get too little or have it provided in tawdry, demeaning conditions and in ways which turn them into dependent caricatures of their potentially creative, self-reliant selves.

Worst of all, the welfare state inflicts damaging levels of moral and psychological harm on its supposed beneficiaries. It has seduced the British people away from their natural independence of spirit and their traditional commitment to hard work, honesty and high standards.

Source: *The Sunday Times*, 31 October 1993

1 Why do we seek equality?

Equality, equity and efficiency

Throughout this book, the assumption has been made that equality is an objective for which to strive. Moving towards a more equal distribution of income and opportunity is closely related to the issue of equity, which has widely differing interpretations. These include:

- Income should be distributed equally.
- People should have what they need.
- No one should fall below a minimum standard of living.
- People should get what they deserve.
- Equal opportunities will result in equity.
- A system agreed by all will result in equity.

Trade-offs

The point of view of each individual depends on his or her political standpoint, but each has a trade-off with other objectives such as economic growth, efficiency and liberty.

The six points all lend themselves to further comment or question:

- Can it be done?
- What incentive does it provide to be innovative/work hard?
- A roof over your head or a holiday in the sun? Who decides?
- Oh dear, what *do* we deserve?
- Is everyone in a position to make the most of opportunities?
- There have been some notable examples in the past of systems agreed by 'everyone'.

There are of course, many more possible questions and comments. Each opinion has its costs and benefits. It is important to weigh these against each other in order to draw conclusions about their relative merits.

The marginal social cost is the additional cost to society of a particular decision. It includes both the costs to the individual and those that have to be met by the government or others who are indirectly affected. The marginal social benefits are the additional benefits to society that result from a particular decision. As with costs, they include the direct benefits plus those that result indirectly.

Neither is always easy to calculate accurately, but an attempt at such evaluation gives a broad indication of the effects of a scheme or policy. By carrying out such work, the areas that will be affected can be identified and the impact recorded. This assists in examining the efficiency of a project, whether in the public or private sector. At the

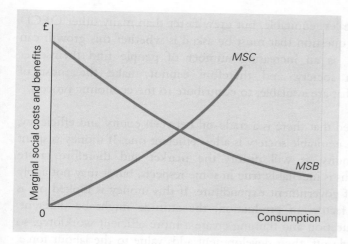

Figure 5.1 Marginal social cost and benefit

Circular flow

point where marginal social cost equals marginal social benefit, efficiency can be achieved, as shown in Figure 5.1. Strategies to reduce inequalities will all have costs and benefits, so if they are to be evaluated effectively these must be investigated carefully to judge whether the additional cost will generate a greater benefit.

In this sphere, the calculation of costs and benefits becomes increasingly difficult. The poorest families in both the developed and developing world suffer social exclusion through deprivation. They cannot participate in society, because they do not have the material possessions or access to elements of the country's culture which would allow them to stay involved. This problem is, in many ways, worse in the developed world, because family units are no longer extensive, having lost the multi-generational pattern of previous centuries, and therefore there is only the state to fall back on for support. In the developing world, unemployment, for example, may be hidden because family members will be absorbed into farming family land, even if the rewards are more thinly spread.

Calculating the cost of social exclusion is difficult, wherever it takes place, yet it has a serious effect on an individual's ability to retain or regain a self-supporting position in the world.

Equality and macroeconomic success

The debate about the role of equality in the process of growth is based on two opposing arguments. The first suggests that inequality stimulates growth because the wealth is in the hands of the few and their savings can be used to finance investment. The alternative view is that the improving economic position of the poor assists the process of growth by allowing more of the population to save and therefore generate funds that will become available for investment. The second argument is starting to hold sway, as the World Bank has shown that there is little connection between degrees of inequality and the speed of growth. The initial impetus for economic growth in developing countries often comes from overseas in the form of aid or foreign direct investment. Government borrowing, as many countries have learned to their cost, has also been significant in the process. The maintenance of growth will, however, be assisted by savings from internal sources. In the developed world the picture becomes more complex. During the 1980s the UK became less equitable, but grew faster than many other OECD members. The question that must be asked is whether this growth can be maintained, as an increasing number of people find themselves excluded from society, and therefore cannot make the most of opportunities that are available, to contribute to the economic process.

It is often argued that there is a trade-off between equity and efficiency, because a more equitable society is a less efficient one. If money is spent on creating equity, it will distort the market and therefore create inefficiency. This is inevitably true in some respects, but it may not apply to all sectors of government expenditure. If this money is looked on as investment in factors of production, the attitude might be different. Healthcare, education and training create a more efficient workforce, so instead of a trade-off, their development adds value to the labour force. The costs and benefits of such policies provide information about how much is worth spending. This type of data can only provide a guide to decision making, because the figures obtained will not be definitive.

Marginal social costs and benefits

National income accounts

In the whole area of income distribution, comparisons are difficult to make because, although there are international data, their comparability is not always reliable. Many countries have no systematic collection mechanisms, so the data presented may have been gathered for another purpose, perhaps in a small sample; they are only an approximation of the true picture. Data showing income distribution may be based on per capita household income or total household income. In countries where large families are the norm, the latter will distort the picture. If these data are not available at all, the information may have been derived from expenditure data. To complicate the picture further, countries that still have a significant proportion of their population living in rural communities may show a distorted picture. Farming families will eat some of the crops they produce. This will, therefore, not appear in either their income or expenditure, so they may be in a relatively better position compared to their urban counterparts.

2 Inside inequality

Lorenz curve

Inequality does not result simply from an unequal income distribution, but also from lack of opportunity and access. An inability to take up educational courses or lack of access to healthcare, for example, has a myriad of impacts. A society in which everyone can benefit from higher education may be much more equitable than one in which it is only open to the children of graduates. Not only are individuals given opportunities to increase their future incomes but society as a whole benefits because resources are being used more efficiently.

Health

Mobility of labour

The article below from the *Washington Post* explains how the need for accessibility to healthcare affects the decisions people make about their working lives and, even more seriously, how that need may affect the decisions that others make about them. The provision of healthcare has become a major subject for debate throughout the developed world, because costs have risen faster than in other sectors. The problems expressed in the article reflect the difficulties faced in countries where medical care is provided mainly by the private sector. Insurance generally has an inflationary effect on prices, as the cost of car repairs demonstrates effectively. The desire for legal redress in American society has also led to substantial increases in costs, because doctors must pay extremely high insurance premiums for protection against making a mistake.

The new definition of poverty: no health insurance

TWO years ago, Jeff and Cynthia Wilkerson decided that it was the perfect time to have a baby. He had just gotten a job as an art director at an ad agency, and it offered 'the best health cover we ever had – no deductibles' Jeff recalls.

Five months into Cynthia's pregnancy, Jeff, 31, was laid off. He was able to find another job in a matter of weeks. But his wife's pregnancy wasn't covered under his new employer's health insurance plan because it was deemed a pre-existing condition – a designation which insurers are resorting to with increasing regularity to contain their costs.

The Wilkersons' son Dylan was born with a defective heart. The couple have been through a harassing odyssey ever since to make sure that they have insurance to cover his medical bills, which have already run into six figures. They have managed to pull it off so far but in the process their premiums tripled to $450 a month – making it impossible to make ends meet on Jeff's $28,000-a-year salary. They've fallen $3,000 in debt on credit cards, had to borrow from Jeff's mother to pay their taxes last year and even considered declaring bankruptcy.

The Wilkersons are neither unemployed or uninsured or bankrupt. Officially they aren't statistics in this recession. But the perils they've faced in the never-never land where job uncertainty and rising health care costs intersect help explain why this recession has packed more of a wallop – economic as well as psychological – than the statistics suggest.

In 1980 the average family paid $1 out of every $11 of its income in health care – in the form of out of pocket costs, insurance premiums or taxes. By 1991, according to Families USA, an advocacy group pushing for health care reform, the average family was paying $1 out of every $8.50 in health care costs – a 30% increase at a time when real family income was flat.

During the same decade, the number of Americans without insurance grew to 34 million from 24.5 million. And during this recession when nearly one worker out of five went through a spell of unemployment last year alone. Tens of millions more Americans have faced the prospect of losing their cover entirely or having it downgraded.

'To be truly at risk of poverty in our society in the late 20th century is to be without health insurance,' says Joshua Weiner, a health economist at the Brookings Institution.

According to a Washington Post–ABC News survey, 24% of Americans said that either they, or a member of their family had decided to stay put in a job in the last two years primarily because they feared their health benefits wouldn't be as good if they changed jobs.

This hesitancy, dubbed 'job lock', has had an even more ominous cousin – 'jobless lock' – which described the problem of an unemployed worker who has a chronic medical condition or a family member with one, but can't find work because employers don't want their insurance rates to shoot up.

'Most of the reports we have are anecdotal, no one has done research on it, but it stands to reason that when insurance companies are tying employer health insurance costs more closely to the medical risks of the people they employ, employers become discriminating about the people they hire,' Weiner says.

One increasingly popular opt-out for employers is to impose a pre-existing condition exclusion on any medical conditions that new employees bring with them. These exclusions, rare a decade ago, have become the rule rather than the exception now for firms with 25 or fewer employees. Such policies are now moving into firms with 25 to 100 employees. And instead of lapsing after a year, more and more of these exclusions are becoming permanent.

Source: *Washington Post: Weekly Edition*, 3 February 1992

Open Question

Should all healthcare needs be met by government, whatever the cost?

In countries where the state is responsible for the provision of healthcare, the issues are similar because rising costs have to be met from taxation, so there is a trade-off between maintaining services and increasing taxes. It is a debate that is influencing decision making throughout Europe and the rest of the developed world.

In the UK, it is estimated that £5 billion a year is lost through sickness.

- On average, one person in twenty is absent from work for at least one day in any week.
- 800,000 people are not working because of permanent or temporary sickness.
- 100,000 people of working age die every year.

Most of our competitors have a much lower sickness rate. Japanese workers, for example, take two-thirds less sick leave than their UK counterparts. On this premise, improving health would lead to greater efficiency. Most of the deaths, on the other hand, are from causes for which there is no cure. There are, however, socio-economic links with death rates. Lower social classes have a higher probability of dying of certain diseases than do those further up the social ladder.

It appears from recent research that people in affluent societies are now influenced more by their relative economic position than their absolute standard of living. When everyone has reached a threshold that provides basic necessities, the distribution of resources seems to become an important factor in achieving well-being.

In the developing world, there is a strong relationship between life expectancy, infant mortality and income level. Every year 25 million children and young adults die, mainly from preventable causes. This loss has economic effects, as was shown in Sri Lanka by the 10% increase in income that occurred when a malaria eradication programme was carried out. Better food and healthcare, therefore, lead to improved productivity.

The costs to industry and the economy as a whole are expressed by the figures above. What is not included is the effect that poor health has on the future. Evidence from research in the developing world shows a close link between nutrition and educational achievement. Nepalese children demonstrated a strong correlation between height-for-age and school attainment and in the Philippines those with a higher weight-for-height ratio performed better in maths achievement tests. On leaving school, higher attainment will mean that these children will find they are able to take jobs that provide a better standard of living and enable them to contribute more effectively to the development of the country.

To achieve this it is important that developing countries concentrate their healthcare programmes on raising the standards for all the population and not just in the provision of high–tech facilities for the affluent city dwellers. The World Bank has proposed a scheme that would establish a programme to do this. It covers both public health and a minimum level of clinical care. Figure 5.2 looks at the areas which are included and Figure 5.3 looks at the relationship between the costs and the benefits.

To put the programme into practice would require massive increases in spending; a four–fold increase on public health and a two–fold increase on clinical care. In middle-income countries this could be coped with by reducing the services for heart surgery, for example, which are much less cost effective. In low-income countries spending currently stands at $6 a head, so a substantial injection of funds would be required. The education of girls and women is particularly effective, because they apply their new-found skills to improving the diet and healthcare of their families.

Figure 5.2 Healthcare for the developing world

Public health	Clinical services
Immunisation for children	Prenatal and delivery care
School-based health services	Family planning
Campaigns to reduce smoking	Tuberculosis care
Campaigns to reduce alcohol consumption	Childhood diseases
Information about nutrition	Simple care for sexually transmitted diseases
Information about family planning	Hospital-based emergency care if resources are available
Aids prevention	

Source: World Bank, *World Development Report*, 1993

Figure 5.3 The costs and benefits

Country group and package component	Cost per capita ($ per year)	Total cost ($bn)	Reduction in disease (%)
Low-income countries	12	22	32
Public health	4	8	8
Essential clinical services	8	14	24
Middle-income countries	22	26	15
Public health	7	8	4
Essential clinical services	15	18	11
All developing countries	15	62	25
Public health	5	21	6
Essential clinical services	10	41	19

Source: World Bank, *World Development Report*, 1993

Human capital

Efficiency

A more equitable distribution of income combined with good healthcare provision appears to create a more healthy and effective population in both the developed and developing world. To achieve this in the latter will require considerable assistance from the rest of the world. Education is obviously an important element of the process, whatever the stage of development.

Education

Education affects productivity and growth in several ways. An improvement in education allows people to absorb information faster and apply their learning more effectively. As industry becomes increasingly dependent on technology, the skills of flexibility and adaptability, which are developed by education, give people an advantage and assist in the growth of the economy. This improves their ability to meet the needs of their families and raise their standard of living. They become more innovative and gain confidence, and this enables them to make better decisions in relation to both home and work. In the previous section, for example, it was demonstrated that government spending would be used to best advantage if the population were well informed.

The data in Figure 5.4 show how wages can rise from one more year of schooling. Assuming that there is a relationship between schooling and productivity or the type of work that is available to a person with more education, this reflects the benefits both to the economy and the individual. The countries and the categories are rather varied, but this reflects the nature of the data available when investigating such fields.

Figure 5.4 Education and wages

Country	% increase in wages		
	Male	**Mixed**	**Female**
Côte d'Ivoire		21	
Ghana		5	
Indonesia	8		12
Peru	8		8
Malaysia	16		18
Nicaragua	10		13
Philippines			18
Thailand	7		25
France			11
USA: whites	6		7
blacks	5		11

Source: World Bank, *World Development Report*, 1991

It has already been mentioned that providing health education for girls has a significant effect on nutrition and well-being. The same is true of general education. In countries where there is still a substantial gender differential in education, less benefit is gained by raising the standard for males. Figure 5.5 shows primary school enrolment rates for males in 1965 compared with infant mortality rates for their children and fertility rates in 1985. The top line in each diagram shows countries with a wide gap between the education of girls and boys, while the bottom line shows countries with a small gap. The small gap leads to lower infant mortality and a reduced birth rate.

Figure 5.5 The effect of the gender gap in education on infant mortality and total fertility

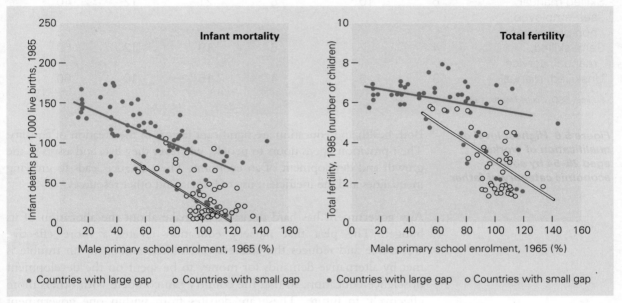

Source: World Bank, *World Development Report*, 1991

Entrepreneurship has been discussed as a factor that leads to increased growth. There is evidence that improving access to education encourages more people to establish businesses. To be successful they need to be prepared to take risks, to organise themselves and others and to plan ahead. Without adequate education, these tasks would either seem daunting or a recipe for disaster.

Multiplier effect

In Britain an individual's final level of educational attainment is closely linked to that of his or her parents. Figure 5.6 shows how the children of professional parents are considerably more likely to be educated to degree level than are others. Although the pattern has changed in the last 30 years, it still suggests that the UK is not making the best use of its young people. The status attached to academic rather than vocational qualifications has been responsible, to a large extent, for this shortcoming, so the development of work-related courses should help to change the balance. Higher levels of educational attainment have a spiral effect on the population because, as the data show, a child's future depends greatly on parents' achievements.

	Degree	Other higher qualification	A level	GCSE grade C+	GCSE grade C–	None %
Professional	32	19	15	19	4	7
Employer/managers	17	15	13	24	9	19
Intermediate, lower non-manual	17	18	12	24	7	18
Skilled manual, self-employed, non-professional	6	10	8	21	12	40
Semi-skilled, manual, service	4	7	6	19	12	50
Unskilled, manual	3	5	4	15	10	60

Source: CSO, *Social Trends*, 1993

Figure 5.6 Highest level of qualification of workers aged 25–54 by socio-economic category of father

Both health and education are significant factors in the creation of equality. Their provision opens doors to people, wherever they live, and assists in the growth and development of an economy. Their absence leads to growing inequalities and the inefficient use of human and other resources.

Any government has hard decisions to make about the allocation of its budget. The plea that nursery education creates a more effective workforce and reduces the chances of children ending up in trouble is met by alternative demands for money to be spent on the development of science education, so that the country can compete with others more effectively in future. These are debates from within one government department. Choices have to be made about the allocation of resources between departments. The evaluation of such decisions depends on political points of view such as the desire for equity or efficiency.

3 Achieving equality: in a national context

Government strategies

Ghana faces a more extreme form of the problems that confront all developing countries when seeking growth and improved conditions for their population. Much of the rich world has had systems that redistribute income to ensure greater equality for many years, but these are only just being established in the developing world. Privatisation and the use of incentives has become a feature of all countries in the process of growth and the search for greater efficiency.

Ghana: edging forward

In Ghana, where the average income per head is $400, 42% of the population live in absolute poverty. Urban life is, on the whole, worse than rural life. Almost 60% of town dwellers earn less than is necessary to keep body and soul together, whereas in the countryside the figure falls to 37%. An estimate suggests that it would take ten years at a growth rate of 8% a year to lift the whole population out of poverty. The current rate is 5%.

The country, whose manufacturing sector is minute, depends on the export of cocoa and gold for its overseas earnings. Only 8% of GDP funds industry through private investment. In Thailand the figure is 32%, which accounts for its rapid growth rate. Ghana lags behind, not only on the economic front but also on the social front. There are still, for example, 20% of children who receive no education at all.

With the help of the IMF, the government hopes that it will achieve the 8% growth rate by the year 2,000. Its strategy is as follows:

- Reduce the role of government through privatisation
- Invest in health and education
- Improve the infrastructure
- Develop the export-led manufacturing sector by offering incentives for investors and elective protection for infant industries; and also by manipulating the banking system to direct foreign exchange to export-oriented customers
- Lure foreign investment from South East Asia into the country with tax holidays, etc.

Progress has been slow, although there has been some interest from transnationals who have met quota problems on exports from South East Asia. Potential investors are holding fire while the country settles into the democracy that was only created in 1992. Control of the economy has also yet to be achieved, as inflation is a problem. Ghana is the only country in sub-Saharan Africa that has achieved so much, but to move from its aid-dependent poverty-stricken state to a role as a competitor in the world market will entail a magnificent leap forward.

Taxation and benefits

Most countries take tax, based on either income or expenditure, from their citizens in order to raise the money for all the services that governments provide. Among these is assistance to relieve poverty among the old, the poor, the unemployed and those who are unable to support themselves.

The welfare state has a variety of redistributional objectives:

1 To relieve poverty and assist the long–term poor
2 Protection against the risk of unemployment, illness or family breakdown
3 Redistribution to groups with greater need
4 Support when the family fails, e.g. women with no pension rights after divorce
5 Smoothing out income level over the life cycle.

The article about the US healthcare system demonstrated how people can fall through the net, which is dominated by the private sector because insurance companies are unwilling to insure individuals who have high–risk factors in their records. The US government has identified this problem and is providing a more supportive system.

In the UK the benefits provided by the state come in cash and kind. Figures 5.7 and 5.8 show how these are distributed.

Figure 5.7 The distribution of cash benefits

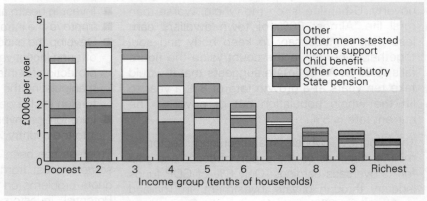

Source: CSO

Figure 5.8 The distribution of benefits in kind

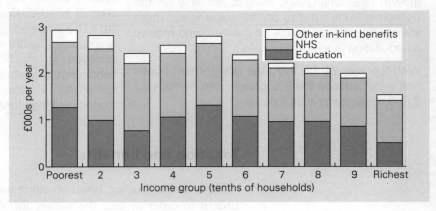

Source: CSO

The graphs show that it is not just the poor who receive assistance from the state. Cash benefits are more clearly directed at the lower deciles, or tenths, of the population, but benefits in kind are more evenly distributed.

The poorest groups receive a range of means-tested benefits, which are not available to the more affluent. Even the cash benefits that are available to all are more significant to the poorest, although it is worth noting that the bottom decile receive less than the second tenth. This is probably because they fail to qualify or do not claim even when entitled.

Benefits in kind in Figure 5.8 still show a concentration on spending at the bottom end, even though it is not as marked as in the previous graph. The inclusion of health and education, which are available to everyone, cause this difference. The rise in the consumption of education towards the fifth decile influences the overall picture.

Both graphs reflect the redistributive value of state provision in both categories of benefits. It must also be remembered that although the rich receive child benefit and other universal assistance, they are also paying taxes, which make them net contributors, rather than net recipients. Figure 5.9 shows who gains and loses from the system.

Figure 5.9 The net gains and losses from benefits and taxes

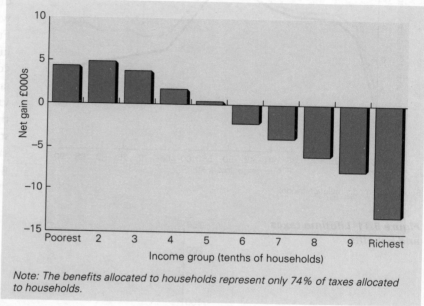

Note: The benefits allocated to households represent only 74% of taxes allocated to households.

Source: CSO

The data presented so far have explained how the welfare state copes with the first four of its objectives. The fifth objective is to even-out lifetime variations in income. Figure 5.10 on page 110 shows this variation, and demonstrates how it is smoothed by benefits and pensions. The original income line rises sharply as people enter the working world and levels out through the period when they are bringing up children. Many people are at their most affluent between their families, leaving home and retirement, at which point income falls sharply. The data on which this is based are from a computer model, called Lifemod, built by the London School of Economics in order to investigate relationships of this type. Net income includes the effects of cash benefits, and final income incorporates benefits in kind. The overall smoothing effect of the welfare system is clearly apparent. The contribution pattern would show the reverse effect, because people would pay into it when income was high and draw out of it when income is low.

The distributional ability of the system can be seen by looking at the amount paid in and received by different sectors of the population over their lifetimes. Even if the rich contribute and the poor draw money

Figure 5.10 The effect of benefits on incomes

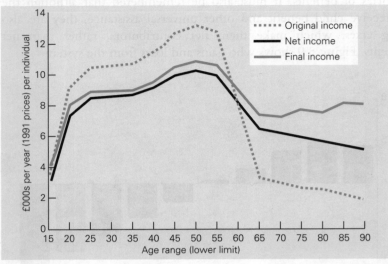

Source: Lifemod simulation model

out in any one year, this may disguise the fact that over a lifetime, there may be no redistribution. If the system merely works as a savings bank, into which money is paid to be drawn out when needed there will be no redistributive effect. Figure 5.11 shows the net lifetime gain to the population compared with the amount of tax that is paid. When these values are compared, about three-quarters of the welfare state is shown to function like a savings bank and the remaining quarter is redistributive.

Figure 5.11 Lifetime taxes and benefits

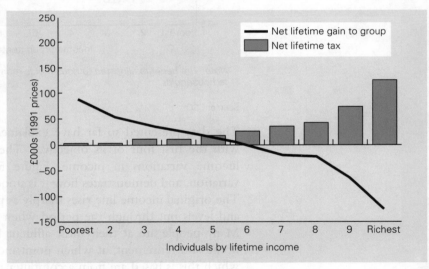

Source: Lifemod simulation model

Can it continue?

The support that has been provided by European countries is beginning to prove problematic. The systems were established when the age structure of the population was very different. An ageing population means that an increasing number of people require the support, not only in cash but also in kind, from a relatively smaller group of wage earners. The state of the German social security system demonstrates the difficulties.

Even Germans can't afford it

AS inventors of social security, Germans are understandably proud of their much imitated system. It provides near universal coverage for health, the dole and pensions. It brought continuity amid upheaval and since 1945, social consensus. To politicians left and right it was untouchable.

No longer. Costs are soaring, benefits dropping. A third of German GDP now goes on social spending. Social insurance contributions (split 50–50 between bosses and workers) amount to almost 40% of gross pay. With such figures in mind, Germans are thinking the unthinkable: can the present welfare state survive? Should it?

Three things have brought matters to a head. First, unification added 17 million citizens, one-third of them getting some form of state relief. East German pension and health rights were taken over. Second, even as Germany pulls out of the deepest recession since 1945, unemployment, now over 4 million, is likely to fall slowly at best, hitting the contribution-based welfare system with a double whammy. Third, Germans are starting to comprehend what the ageing of their population may mean. By 2015, the number of Germans over the age of 65 will rise from 12 million to over 18 million. By 2030 on one estimate, 38% of Germans will be over 60 and 16% under 20. According to the OECD, the present value of future pensions in Germany is 1.6 times current GDP. The government is struggling to trim costs with mixed results.

Figure 5.12 Germany's bursting welfare state

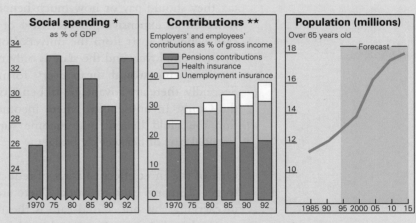

* Including eastern Germany from July 1990   ** Western Germany

Source: *The Economist*, 19 February 1994

Apart from the problems that have arisen through reunification, the rest of Europe faces similar problems. There will not be enough young people to finance pensions for the increasing number of elderly. Eventually pensions would eat up all government spending. One strategy to overcome the problem is to encourage people to opt out of the state system and provide for themselves in the private sector. Much of the population could afford to do so, and the result might be more equitable as it would lead to adequate provision for those for whom there was no alternative. There are benefits in terms of costs, but the American system has demonstrated how private insurance can lead to individuals having no means of buying or providing for their needs, because insurance companies will not cover bad risks.

On the issue of unemployment, governments are seeking to reduce the amount of benefit and duration of its availability in order to reduce expenditure. In the light of the discussion about world trends in unemployment, such policies are likely to worsen inequality. Private insurance is one option that would reduce government expenditure.

More means testing has been advocated as a method of allocating resources to those who need them most, but it is expensive to administer and may deter claimants, who end up being fully dependent on the state rather than using non-means tested benefits to top up their earnings.

Unless the systems for taxes and benefits are unified into a 'tax credit' scheme, it is often difficult for those who have been unemployed and receiving benefit to take jobs without losing out financially. This gap has become known as the poverty trap, and its existence reduces the incentive to take low-paid jobs. A tax credit scheme looks at people's incomes and needs and then makes an overall assessment of how much tax they should pay or how much benefit they should receive. This is, however, an expensive process. Most of the population do not receive cash benefits, apart from the universal ones. Their tax bills are assessed by their employers and the state is only involved in a limited way. A tax credit scheme would mean every form had to be assessed regularly. Secondly, there are advantages in benefits going to different members of the family. In households where income is not shared, a mother may find the child benefit and income support, which she receives, an essential part of her weekly budget.

One of the most effective ways of reducing government expenditure is to get claimants back to work. There are, of course, expenses involved in carrying this out. Child-care is the main need. It is expensive and cannot be taken into account when claims are made or tax is paid.

In order to tackle these problems, governments have to make choices, as there are always trade-offs between alternative strategies. The three interrelated factors that must be considered are:

■ How much are they going to spend?
■ Who are they going to spend it on?
■ Where will the money come from?

In Figure 5.13 the alternatives are spelt out. Each of the three sections shows a spectrum of options from which a government might select. They are interrelated because the amount that is available to spend will determine the number of people who can be helped and therefore how individuals are targeted. On the left side of each section of the diagram are policies that lead to greater welfare spending and less discrimination about who receives benefits. The right side shows policies that reduce welfare spending and target it more specifically. Within each section, there is also a variation from the top to the bottom showing the different strategies.

Figure 5.13 Welfare policy options

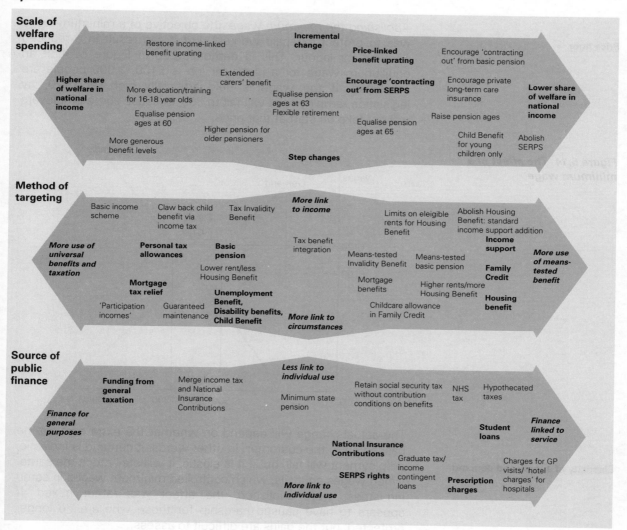

Source: John Hills, *The Future of Welfare*, Joseph Rowntree Foundation, 1993

Incentives

An alternative to giving benefits to those who cannot find a role in the economic system is to remove restrictions and provide incentives in order to encourage growth and, therefore, stimulate employment. These are often referred to as supply side policies, because their objective is to increase output, thus shifting the aggregate supply curve to the right.

They achieve their objective by removing imperfections from the market, often by withdrawing protection from particular groups or assisting others to become more competitive. There is a variety of strategies that can be employed, the effectiveness of which is uncertain:

Price floor

1   *Abolishing the minimum wage:* the objective of a minimum wage was to protect low-paid workers, but it can result in a reduced demand for labour. This is demonstrated in Figure 5.14. If an equilibrium wage for a particular job is £100, 1,000 people are employed. If the wage is held artificially high, at £120, by legislation, employment will fall to 800, because some employers will not take on staff at that price.

Figure 5.14 *The effect of a minimum wage*

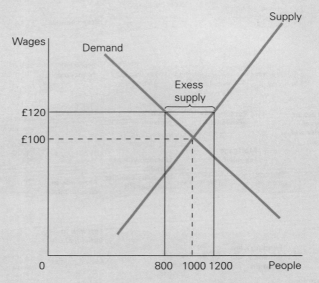

The actual change will depend on whether the extra cost can be passed on to the customer. In other words, if demand is inelastic, employment will fall, but if it is elastic, it will stay much the same. When wages councils, which controlled minimum wages in some industries, were abolished, the effect was rather mixed. It appears to have caused hardship for those who are no longer protected, but the gains are difficult to assess.

Elasticity of supply and demand

2   *Limiting trade union power:* trade unions protect the pay and conditions of work of their members, but by doing so economic theory suggests that they will reduce output and employment in the market as a whole. This occurs because wages are raised above the equilibrium and employment falls. The aggregate supply curve, therefore, shifts to the left. By limiting unions' activities, this can be prevented. The market for labour will become more competitive, so prices will fall and output will rise.

Figure 5.15 The effect of trade unions

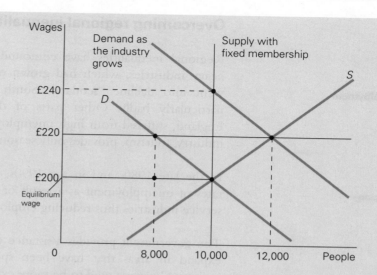

In Figure 5.15, the equilibrium wage is £200, where 10,000 people are employed. After a negotiated pay rise of £20, demand for labour drops to 8,000. By limiting membership, the union will be in a strong position if demand for labour of this type increases. As the demand curve shifts to the right, they are rewarded with a pay rise, which takes the wage to £240 because the supply of members is fixed at 10,000. In a free market, the wage would be £220 and 12,000 people would be employed.

3 *New education and training opportunities:* education and training are key elements in economic growth. By providing schemes that enable more people to take advantage of new opportunities, both individuals and society benefit.

The improved access to education in the developing world has been an important theme in the discussion of equality and growth. It is also of equal relevance to the developed world, where it is essential to make the most of the workforce if a country is to remain competitive. The establishment of appropriate training courses and qualifications, particularly in the vocational fields, will have a significant effect on a country's productivity.

4 *Reducing taxation:* cutting taxes persuades individuals to work harder because they keep a higher percentage of their earnings. Entrepreneurs will take more risks because they will retain more profit. Income, output and employment are generated.

5 *Privatisation:* this tactic has been used everywhere with the aim of increasing efficiency and therefore growth. In some developing countries it has freed the government of responsibility for loss-making activities and therefore allowed increased spending on other projects. The effectiveness may be counteracted, certainly in the short term, if unemployment results from the sale.

Unemployment

Recession

Index numbers

Overcoming regional inequalities

Regional inequalities have confounded the UK economy since the heavy industries, which had grown out of the Industrial Revolution, went into decline. Scotland, South Wales and the North suffered particularly badly. Other parts of the country, such as south-west England, suffered from high unemployment because their predominant industry, tourism, provides only seasonal employment.

In the late 1980s and in the 1990s, south-east England suffered high rates of unemployment as a result of the recession. The downturn hit service industries thus reducing employment considerably.

The government provides assistance to industry planning to set up or expand in areas that have been specifically identified within these regions. Coverage used to be more extensive, but is now targeted.

4 Achieving equality: in a European context

Regional strategies

Within Europe there is a great disparity in levels of development and resulting wealth. In order that countries and regions can compete on a level playing-field, the European Union provides financial assistance. As the UK is a member of the European Union, assistance is available to areas of the country that fall within the EU's objectives. Priority, or Objective 1, regions receive most assistance, because they face the greatest difficulties. Figure 5.16 uses index numbers to show the relative positions of some European cities in terms of GDP per head. Merseyside falls well below the average and is now entitled to Objective 1 assistance. The extent of funding to such areas to the end of the century is shown in Figure 5.17.

Figure 5.16 The rich and poor of Europe

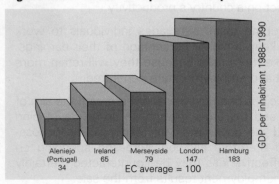

Source: European Parliament

Figure 5.17 Assistance to Europe's regions

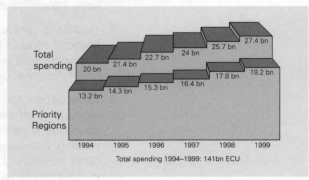

Source: European Parliament

Merseyside

MERSEYSIDE is a proud region, built on an earlier trading and manufacturing prosperity which has suffered heavily in the post-industrial economic restructuring of the past decades.

The decline is most marked in manufacturing industry with some 76,000 jobs lost since 1981. Unemployment on Merseyside, currently at 15%, usually runs at around 50% above the national average.

The region is at a turning point and sees Objective 1 status as offering a unique opportunity to revitalise the economy on the basis of partnership between the EU, central and local government and the private and voluntary sectors.

Investment will concentrate on improving communications and diversifying the economic base with a view to attracting new hi-tech industries. This means cleaning up areas of dereliction, tackling pollution, reversing population decline and improving the city's image, making it an attractive place for tourists, students and investors alike.

Renewed confidence will lead to an increase in small and medium sized enterprises, improved services and job opportunities eventually bringing about a reduction in disparities.

Source: *EP News*, 21 June 1993

Initiatives

The Poverty Action Programme aims to overcome social exclusion. This afflicts long-term unemployed, immigrants, single-parent families, drug addicts or the elderly. Earlier, it was used to describe families whose income levels were so low that they could not participate in society. Exclusion has both social and economic implications; it may preclude attendance at training courses, for example.

In this context, the EU is backing an urban regeneration programme in London's docklands, where unemployment is high and housing conditions are often poor. The programme consists of complementary elements. Training is provided for the long-term unemployed and single parents. Social facilities are being improved, with the provision of additional child-care. Young people from the area are being employed by local builders to carry out a housing renovation scheme. By carrying out these programmes, individuals are being provided with opportunities to re-enter the world of work, from which they were excluded by lack of training or domestic commitments. As a result, inequalities are diminished.

An alternative solution to job shortage

The rise of unemployment on a world-wide basis has called for rethinking about the structure of the average working life. Already most young people continue to study until they are at least 18, if not beyond. The retirement age for many people in corporate pension schemes is falling.

There is a movement to look at the whole picture in order to share out the available work. European socialist parties, for example, are asking for a significantly shorter working week.

5 Achieving equality: in a global context

Strategies for achieving growth and greater equality in the developing world have already been discussed in the contexts of trade and aid. From these sections the problems of redistribution within and between countries has become clear. To some extent the picture can appear as a zero sum game – there can be no winners without losers. If the North gains from global development, the South will lose, and assistance to the South will only be at the cost of the North. If, however, such trade-offs are to be overcome, both countries and groups of countries must look at the global impact of their decisions.

In an ideal situation, growth would lead to equality on a global scale, but at this point politics distorts the picture. Equality in any one country is greatly determined by the allocation decisions made by the government, the UK being a prime example. Few decisions are altruistic, as each country has motives for its attitudes which reflect the political position at home. The GATT agreement, which benefits the developed world more than the developing world, reflects this. Despite this imbalance in outcome, results of the GATT round have opened markets and widened opportunities for world trade.

If the patterns of world trade are going to develop further, the South must be able to take advantage of the opportunities by effective investment in both human and physical capital. This may be resourced by aid, inward investment or the generation of funds from internal sources. Whatever its origin, the plan must be to achieve growth, which will enable a country to compete in world markets. People are crucial to this process and therefore investment in health and education cannot be regarded as a by-product, but as a key factor in the establishment of a healthy growing economy. The World Bank identified widespread education as one of the few policies that the growing countries of South East Asia have in common.

Once the objective of growth is established, the process needs to be monitored carefully. Sustainability will mean that the future is more secure. Countries that allow their environment to be destroyed or permit development that uses raw materials that it fails to replace, will find that growth is short term and the costs may be greater than the benefits. It is tempting for a developing country, which seeks the rapid rewards of growth, to encourage inward investment by accepting lower standards than developed countries. Companies may find this attractive because they have a lower cost base.

The absorption of land into urban areas reduces the supplies on which populations have long been dependent. Firewood, for example, is essential to the livelihoods of millions of people, but is disappearing more quickly than it can be replaced. The result of the destruction of traditional lifestyles can lead to a combination of the pollution of poverty and the pollution of affluence. If the costs are borne by the poor and the benefits by the rich, corrective action can be hard to implement because power is generally in the hands of the latter.

The clauses of NAFTA, which require the same degree of control in Mexico as in the USA, may be a starting point. The desire of the working population of the developed world to protect themselves from competition may be more effective than all the persuasion in the world. Self interest generally seems a powerful motive force.

The debt issue is a restraining factor on several countries and the process of easing the problem would be greatly to their advantage. Every decision that is made has trade-off effects, and winners in one country may create losers in another.

Open Question

Is it important not to create losers in the process of achieving greater equality?

As yet, the effect of inequality on economic growth is not fully understood. Its inter-relationship with other factors that contribute to growth is important, but it appears not to be essential at the outset, as the case studies have shown. An efficient workforce becomes significant as development progresses because of the necessity to compete.

There are many factors involved in achieving greater equality, of which growth is one. Different situations require different solutions, and appropriate strategies must be mixed according to need.

Index